As a Man Thinketh & From Poverty to Power

The Life-Changing Power of Positive Thinking and Self-Mastery

A Modern Translation

Adapted for the Contemporary Reader

James Allen

Table of Contents

Preface - Message to the Reader

Rebuilding the Greatest Library in Human History

Thousands of years ago, the Library of Alexandria was the heart of global knowledge — a sanctuary where the wisdom of every known civilization was gathered and shared freely.

And then, it was lost.

Now, we're rebuilding it — and you are invited to join us.

At the Library of Alexandria, we've set out to make every book available to *every person on Earth* — not just in print, but in every language, every format, and for every reader.

Here's how we do it:

- **Deluxe Print Editions at True Printing Cost** - Order any book as a high-quality paperback, elegant hardcover, or stunning boxset — and only pay what it costs to print. No markups. No middlemen.

- **Unlimited Access to the Greatest Works** - Enjoy thousands of timeless classics — from Plato to Shakespeare to Tolstoy — in beautiful, modern eBook and audiobook editions. Read and listen without limits — for every reader, everywhere.

- **Modern Translations for Every Language & Dialect** - We're reimagining the classics in clear, accessible language — and translating them into every dialect imaginable. Everyone deserves to understand humanity's greatest ideas.

When you visit **LibraryofAlexandria.com**, you're not just accessing books — you're joining a global movement to restore, preserve, and share the wisdom of civilization.

Join us today at LibraryofAlexandria.com

Together, we'll ensure the light of human wisdom never fades again.

With gratitude,
The Modern Library of Alexandria Team

Visit:

www.libraryofalexandria.com

Or scan the code below:

1

Introduction

*"Mind is the Master power that moulds and makes, And Man is
Mind, and evermore he takes
The tool of Thought, and, shaping what he wills, Brings
forth a thousand joys, a thousand ills:— He thinks in
secret, and it comes to pass: Environment is but his looking-
glass."*

~ James Allen

This little book, which is the result of meditation and experience, is not meant to be a complete work on the often-discussed topic of the power of thought. Instead, it aims to inspire rather than explain, with the goal of encouraging men and women to discover and understand the truth that— "They themselves are makers of themselves."

This is because of the thoughts they choose and nurture. The mind is the master-weaver, shaping both the inner garment of character and the outer garment of circumstance. Although people may have woven their lives in ignorance and pain before, they can now weave in enlightenment and happiness.

James Allen
Broad Park Avenue,
Ilfracombe,

As a Man Thinketh

James Allen

CHAPTER 1

THOUGHT AND CHARACTER

The saying "As a man thinks in his heart, so is he" describes not only a person's entire being but also covers every aspect of their life. A person is truly what they think, as their character is the sum total of all their thoughts.

Just as a plant grows from a seed and cannot exist without it, every action of a person comes from hidden seeds of thought and could not happen without them. This applies to actions that seem "spontaneous" and "unpremeditated" as much as it does to those that are planned.

Action is the blossom of thought, and joy and suffering are its fruits. Thus, a person harvests the sweet and bitter outcomes of their own cultivation.

"Thought in the mind has made us what we are. By thought was wrought and built. If a man's mind has evil thoughts, pain comes to him just as the wheel follows the ox. If one endures in purity of thought, joy follows him like his own shadow—sure."

A person grows by law, not by artificial means, and cause and effect are as absolute and unchanging in the hidden realm of thought as they are in the world of visible and material things. A noble and godlike character is not a gift or a result of chance but is the natural result of consistent right thinking and the effect of dwelling on godlike thoughts for a long time. In the same way, an ignoble and beastly character results from continually harboring lowly thoughts.

A person is made or unmade by themselves. In the workshop of thought, they create the weapons that can destroy themselves or the tools with which they build heavenly mansions of joy, strength, and peace. By choosing the right thoughts and applying them correctly, a person rises to divine perfection; by misusing and wrongly applying thoughts, they fall below the level of a beast. Between these two extremes are all the levels of character, and a person is their creator and master.

Of all the beautiful truths about the soul that have been discovered and brought to light in this age, none is more uplifting or full of divine promise and confidence than this: that a person is the master of their thoughts, the shaper of their character, and the creator of their conditions, environment, and destiny.

As a being of power, intelligence, and love, and the ruler of their own thoughts, a person holds the key to every situation and possesses within themselves the transformative and regenerative ability to become what they desire.

A person is always the master, even in their weakest and most abandoned state. However, in their weakness and degradation, they are a foolish master who mismanages their "household." When they begin to reflect on their condition and diligently search for the Law upon which their being is founded, they become the wise master, directing their energies with intelligence and shaping their thoughts to achieve positive outcomes. This is the conscious master, and a person can only become this by discovering within themselves the laws of thought. This discovery is entirely a matter of application, self-analysis, and experience.

Gold and diamonds are obtained only through much searching and mining, and a person can find every truth related to their being if they dig deep into the mine of their soul. They can prove that they are the maker of their character, the shaper of their life, and the builder of their destiny if they watch, control, and change their thoughts, observing their effects on themselves, on others, and on their life and circumstances. By linking cause and effect through patient practice and investigation, and using every experience, even the most trivial, everyday occurrences, as a means of gaining self-knowledge, they gain understanding, wisdom, and power. In this pursuit, like no other, the law is absolute that "He that seeks, finds; and to him that knocks, it shall be opened;" for only through patience, practice, and constant persistence can a person enter the Door of the Temple of Knowledge.

• • •

CHAPTER 2

EFFECT OF THOUGHT
ON CIRCUMSTANCES

A man's mind can be compared to a garden, which can be carefully tended or allowed to grow wild. But whether you take care of it or not, it will produce something. If you don't plant good seeds, weeds will grow in abundance.

Just as a gardener takes care of his garden, keeping it free from weeds and growing the flowers and fruits he wants, a person can tend the garden of their mind by removing wrong, useless, and impure thoughts and nurturing right, useful, and pure ones. By doing this, a person eventually realizes that they are the master gardener of their soul and the director of their life. They also discover the laws of thought within themselves and understand more clearly how thoughts shape their character, circumstances, and destiny.

Thought and character are connected, and since character shows itself through environment and circumstances, a person's outer conditions will always be related to their inner state. This doesn't mean that a person's circumstances at any moment fully reveal their entire character, but that these circumstances are deeply linked to some essential thought within them and are necessary for their growth at that time.

Every person is where they are because of the law of their being. The thoughts they have built into their character have brought them there, and nothing in their life happens by chance. Everything is the result of a law that cannot make mistakes. This is true for both those who feel out of harmony with their surroundings and those who are content.

As a growing and evolving being, a person is where they are to learn and grow. As they learn the spiritual lesson in any circumstance, it passes away and makes room for new ones.

People are affected by circumstances as long as they believe they are controlled by outside conditions. But when they realize they are a creative force and can control the inner seeds and soil from which circumstances grow, they become the true master of themselves.

Anyone who has practiced self-control and self-purification knows that circumstances arise from thought. They notice that changes in their circumstances occur in exact proportion to their mental changes. When someone sincerely works to fix their character's flaws and makes quick and noticeable progress, they often go through a series of changes.

The soul attracts what it secretly harbors, loves, and fears. It reaches the heights of its aspirations and falls to the level of its unrefined desires, and circumstances are how the soul receives its due.

Every thought planted in the mind takes root, grows into action, and bears fruit in the form of opportunity and circumstance. Good thoughts bring good fruit; bad thoughts bring bad fruit.

The external world shapes itself to the internal world of thought. Both pleasant and unpleasant conditions ultimately benefit the individual. As a harvester of his own crop, a person learns through both suffering and joy.

By following the desires, aspirations, and thoughts that dominate him—whether pursuing fleeting fantasies or steadfastly following the path of high endeavor—a person ultimately reaches their fulfillment in the outer conditions of their life. Everywhere, the laws of growth and adjustment apply.

A person does not end up in poverty or jail because of fate or circumstance but by following lowly thoughts and desires. Similarly, a pure-minded person does not suddenly commit a crime due to external forces; the criminal thought was nurtured in their heart long before, and opportunity revealed its power. Circumstance does not make the man; it reveals him to himself. One cannot fall into vice without vicious inclinations or rise into virtue without nurturing virtuous aspirations. As the lord of thought, a person makes himself, shaping his environment and destiny. Even at birth, the soul attracts the conditions that reflect its purity and impurity, strength and weakness.

People do not attract what they want but what they are. Their whims and ambitions are thwarted, but their innermost thoughts and desires are fulfilled, whether good or bad. The "divinity that shapes our ends" is within us; it is our very self. Only a person can chain themselves. Thought and action are the jailers of fate, imprisoning us when base and liberating us when noble. A person does not receive what they wish and pray for, but what they earn. Their wishes and prayers are fulfilled only when they align with their thoughts and actions.

In light of this truth, what does it mean to "fight against circumstances"? It means continually opposing an external effect while nurturing and maintaining its cause in one's heart. This cause may be a conscious vice or an unconscious weakness, but it hinders progress and calls for remedy.

People want to improve their circumstances but are unwilling to improve themselves, so they remain stuck. A person who does not shy away from self-sacrifice will always achieve their goals. This applies to both earthly and heavenly pursuits. Even someone who wants to become wealthy must be willing to make personal sacrifices to succeed. How much more must one do to achieve a balanced and strong life?

Consider a man who is desperately poor. He wants to improve his surroundings and comfort but shirks his work and thinks he is justified in deceiving his employer due to low wages. Such a man does not understand the basic principles of prosperity and is not only unable to rise out of poverty but attracts deeper misery by indulging in lazy and deceptive thoughts.

Or consider a wealthy man who suffers from a persistent disease caused by gluttony. He is willing to spend large sums to cure it but won't give up his excessive desires. He wants to enjoy rich food and good health, but he is unfit for health because he hasn't learned the basics of a healthy life.

Then there is the employer who cuts wages to increase profits, not realizing he is setting himself up for failure. When he faces bankruptcy in both reputation and wealth, he blames circumstances, not knowing he is the sole author of his condition.

These examples illustrate that a person often unconsciously creates their circumstances. While aiming for a good outcome, they undermine their success by nurturing thoughts and desires that don't align with their goals. Readers can trace the action of thought in their minds and lives and see how external circumstances cannot serve as the sole basis for reasoning.

Circumstances are complex, thought is deeply rooted, and the conditions of happiness vary greatly among individuals. A man's entire soul condition, though it may be known to himself, cannot be judged by another based solely on his external life. A man may be honest in some areas yet suffer privations; a man may be dishonest in some areas yet acquire wealth. The conclusion that one fails due to honesty and the other succeeds due to dishonesty results from superficial judgment, assuming the dishonest man is entirely corrupt and the honest man is entirely virtuous. Deeper knowledge and experience show such judgments to be false. The dishonest man may have virtues the other lacks, and the honest man may have vices the other is free from. The honest man reaps the rewards of his good thoughts and actions and suffers from his vices. The dishonest man similarly experiences his own suffering and happiness.

It's comforting to human vanity to believe one suffers due to virtue, but until a man removes every bitter and impure thought from his mind and cleanses his soul of sin, he cannot declare that his suffering is due to his good qualities. Before reaching supreme perfection, he will find the Great Law of Justice operating in his mind and life, which does not give good for evil or evil for good. With this knowledge, he will look back on his past ignorance and blindness and know that his life is and always has been justly ordered and that all his past experiences, good and bad, were the fair outcomes of his evolving self.

Good thoughts and actions never produce bad results, and bad thoughts and actions never produce good results. Just as corn cannot produce anything but corn and nettles nothing but nettles, this law is understood in the natural world. Still, few understand it in the mental and moral world, though it operates just as consistently there.

Suffering always results from wrong thoughts. It indicates that an individual is out of harmony with themselves and the law of their being. The sole purpose of suffering is to purify and remove all that is useless and impure. Suffering ceases for the pure. There is no reason to burn gold once the impurities have been removed, and a perfectly pure and enlightened being cannot suffer.

The circumstances a man encounters with suffering result from his own mental disharmony. The circumstances a man encounters with blessedness result from his own mental harmony. Blessedness, not material possessions, measures right thought; wretchedness, not a lack of material possessions, measures wrong thought. A man may be cursed and rich, or blessed and poor. Blessedness and riches only come together when riches are rightly and wisely used. A poor man only falls into wretchedness when he sees his situation as an unjust burden.

Poverty and indulgence are the two extremes of wretchedness, both equally unnatural and the result of mental disorder. A man is only rightly conditioned when he is happy, healthy, and prosperous, and happiness, health, and prosperity result from harmoniously aligning his inner self with his surroundings.

A person begins to truly live when they stop complaining and blaming others and start searching for the hidden justice that governs their life. As they align their mind with this justice, they stop blaming others for their condition and build themselves up with strong and noble thoughts. They stop fighting against circumstances and begin to use them to progress faster and discover their inner powers and possibilities.

Law, not chaos, is the dominant principle in the universe; justice, not injustice, is the soul of life; and righteousness, not corruption, is the force behind the spiritual governance of the world. This means that by aligning himself with righteousness, a man will find that the universe aligns with him. As he changes his thoughts towards things and people, things and people will change towards him.

The truth of this is in every person, allowing for easy investigation through introspection and self-analysis. Let a person radically change their thoughts, and they will be amazed at the rapid transformation it brings to their material conditions. People think thoughts can be kept secret, but they can't; thoughts quickly crystallize into habits, which solidify into circumstances. Bestial thoughts lead to habits of drunkenness and sensuality, which result in poverty and disease. Impure thoughts lead to habits of confusion and distraction, resulting in adverse circumstances. Fearful, doubtful, and indecisive thoughts lead to weak habits, resulting in failure and dependence. Lazy thoughts lead to habits of uncleanliness and dishonesty, resulting in poverty. Hateful and critical thoughts lead to habits of accusation and violence, resulting in injury and persecution. Selfish thoughts lead to self- seeking habits, resulting in distressing circumstances. Conversely, beautiful thoughts lead to habits of grace and kindness, resulting in pleasant circumstances. Pure thoughts lead to habits of self- control, resulting in peace. Courageous and self-reliant thoughts lead to successful and free circumstances. Energetic thoughts lead to habits of cleanliness and industry, resulting in pleasant circumstances. Gentle and forgiving thoughts lead to protective circumstances. Loving and selfless thoughts lead to self- forgetfulness habits, resulting in prosperity and true riches.

A particular train of thought, whether good or bad, will inevitably produce results on character and circumstances. While a person cannot directly choose their circumstances, they can choose their thoughts and, by doing so, indirectly shape their circumstances.

Nature helps everyone fulfill the thoughts they most encourage, and opportunities arise that will quickly bring good and evil thoughts to the surface.

Let a person abandon sinful thoughts, and the world will soften towards them and be ready to help. Let them discard weak thoughts, and opportunities will arise to aid their strong resolves.

Let them nurture good thoughts, and no hard fate will bind them to wretchedness and shame. The world is your kaleidoscope, and its ever-changing patterns are the carefully adjusted pictures of your thoughts.

"So You will be what you will to be;

Let failure find its false content In that

poor word, 'environment,' But spirit

scorns it, and is free.

"It masters time, it conquers space; It cowes

that boastful trickster, Chance,

And bids the tyrant Circumstance Uncrown,

and fill a servant's place. "The human Will,

that force unseen, The offspring of a deathless

Soul, Can hew a way to any goal,

Though walls of granite intervene. "Be not

impatient in delays

But wait as one who understands; When

spirit rises and commands The gods are

ready to obey."

• • •

CHAPTER 3

EFFECT OF THOUGHT ON HEALTH AND THE BODY

The body serves the mind. It follows what the mind thinks, whether those thoughts are intentionally chosen or come automatically. When the mind is filled with negative or unlawful thoughts, the body quickly falls into sickness and decay. On the other hand, when the mind is full of happy and beautiful thoughts, the body becomes youthful and healthy.

Just like circumstances, disease and health are rooted in thought. Sickly thoughts show up in a sickly body. Fearful thoughts can kill a person as quickly as a bullet, and they are constantly affecting thousands of people, even if not as suddenly. Those who fear disease are the ones who often get it. Anxiety weakens the entire body and makes it susceptible to disease, while impure thoughts, even if not acted upon physically, will eventually harm the nervous system.

Strong, pure, and happy thoughts build up the body with strength and grace. The body is sensitive and responds to the thoughts it receives, and habitual thoughts will have their effects, whether good or bad.

People will continue to have impure and unhealthy bodies as long as they have unclean thoughts. A clean heart leads to a clean life and a healthy body. A polluted mind leads to a corrupt life and an unhealthy body. Thought is the source of action, life, and expression; make the source pure, and everything will be pure.

Changing one's diet won't help if a person doesn't change their thoughts. When a person purifies their thoughts, they no longer desire unhealthy food.

Pure thoughts lead to clean habits. A so-called saint who does not wash is not a saint. A person who strengthens and purifies their thoughts does not need to worry about harmful germs.

To protect your body, guard your mind. To renew your body, beautify your mind. Thoughts of malice, envy, disappointment, and despair rob the body of its health and beauty. A sour face is not an accident; it is created by sour thoughts. Wrinkles are caused by foolishness, passion, and pride.

I know a woman who is ninety-six with the bright, innocent face of a young girl. I know a man who is much younger, yet his face is distorted by passion and discontent. The difference is that the woman has a sweet and sunny disposition, while the man has been consumed by negative emotions.

Just as you cannot have a sweet and healthy home without letting in air and sunshine, you cannot have a strong body and a bright, happy face without letting thoughts of joy, goodwill, and calmness into your mind.

On the faces of the elderly, some wrinkles are made by sympathy, others by pure thought, and others by passion. Who cannot tell the difference? For those who have lived righteously, old age is calm, peaceful, and gently mellowed, like a setting sun. I recently saw a philosopher on his deathbed. He was not old, except in years. He died as sweetly and peacefully as he lived.

Cheerful thoughts are the best medicine for curing the body's ills, and goodwill is the best comfort for dispelling grief and sorrow. Living with thoughts of ill will, cynicism, suspicion, and envy is like being in a prison you've built yourself. But thinking well of others, being cheerful, and finding the good in everyone—such unselfish thoughts are like the gates to heaven. Living each day with thoughts of peace toward all creatures will bring peace to the person who has them.

• • •

CHAPTER 4

THOUGHT AND PURPOSE

Until thought is linked with purpose, there can be no intelligent accomplishment. Most people let their thoughts drift aimlessly through life. Aimlessness is a vice, and anyone who wants to avoid catastrophe and destruction must not let it continue.

Those who lack a central purpose in their lives are easily overwhelmed by worries, fears, troubles, and self-pity, all of which are signs of weakness. These lead to failure, unhappiness, and loss just as surely as deliberately planned sins, though by a different path, because weakness cannot survive in a universe where power is constantly growing.

A person should form a clear purpose in their heart and work towards achieving it. This purpose should become the center of their thoughts. It could be a spiritual ideal or a worldly goal, depending on their nature at the time, but whatever it is, they should consistently focus their mental energy on the goal they have set. This purpose should be their highest priority, and they should dedicate themselves to reaching it, not letting their thoughts wander off into temporary fancies, desires, and imaginings. This is the key to self-control and true concentration of thought. Even if they fail repeatedly to achieve their purpose (as they inevitably will until they overcome their weaknesses), the strength of character they gain will be a true measure of their success. This will become a new starting point for future power and triumph.

Those who are not ready to grasp a great purpose should focus their thoughts on performing their duties flawlessly, no matter how unimportant their tasks may seem. Only in this way can they gather and focus their thoughts, develop resolution and energy, and once this is achieved, there is nothing that cannot be accomplished.

Even the weakest soul, knowing its own weaknesses and believing the truth that strength can only be developed through effort and practice, will begin to exert itself. By adding effort to effort, patience to patience, and strength to strength, it will never stop growing and will eventually become divinely strong.

Just as a physically weak person can become strong through careful and patient training, so can a person with weak thoughts make them strong by practicing right thinking.

To get rid of aimlessness and weakness and to start thinking with purpose is to join the ranks of those strong individuals who only see failure as one of the paths to achievement, who make every condition serve them, and who think strongly, attempt fearlessly, and accomplish masterfully.

Once a person has conceived a purpose, they should mentally map out a direct path to its achievement, without looking to the right or the left. Doubts and fears should be strictly avoided; they are disruptive elements that break up the straight line of effort, making it crooked, ineffective, and useless. Thoughts of doubt and fear have never accomplished anything and never will. They always lead to failure. Purpose, energy, and the power to act disappear when doubt and fear creep in.

The will to act comes from knowing that we can act. Doubt and fear are the greatest enemies of knowledge, and anyone who encourages them or fails to eliminate them hinders themselves at every step.

A person who has conquered doubt and fear has conquered failure. Every thought they have is connected to power, and they face all difficulties bravely and overcome them wisely. Their purposes are planted at the right time, and they bloom and produce fruit, which does not fall prematurely to the ground.

Thought that is fearlessly linked to purpose becomes a creative force: anyone who knows this is ready to become something higher and stronger than a mere bundle of wavering thoughts and fluctuating sensations; anyone who does this has become the conscious and intelligent wielder of their mental powers.

• • •

CHAPTER 5

THE THOUGHT-FACTOR
IN ACHIEVEMENT

Everything a person achieves or fails to achieve is the direct result of their own thoughts. In a universe that is justly ordered, where any loss of balance would mean total destruction, individual responsibility must be absolute. A person's weaknesses and strengths, purity and impurity, are their own, not someone else's. They are created by themselves, not by others, and can only be changed by themselves, never by another person. Their condition is also their own, not someone else's. Their suffering and happiness come from within. As they think, so they are; as
they continue to think, so they remain.

A strong person cannot help a weaker one unless that weaker person is willing to be helped, and even then, the weak person must become strong on their own; they must develop the strength they admire in another through their own efforts. No one but themselves can change their condition.

People have often thought and said, "Many people are slaves because one is an oppressor; let's hate the oppressor." However, there is now a growing tendency among some to reverse this judgment and say, "One person is an oppressor because many are slaves; let's despise the slaves."

The truth is that both oppressor and slave are cooperating in ignorance, and while they seem to harm each other, they are actually harming themselves. Perfect Knowledge understands the law at work in the weakness of the oppressed and the misused power of the oppressor; perfect Love, seeing the suffering that both states bring, condemns neither; perfect Compassion embraces both oppressor and oppressed.

Anyone who has conquered weakness and let go of all selfish thoughts belongs to neither oppressor nor oppressed. They are free.

A person can only rise, conquer, and achieve by lifting up their thoughts. They can only remain weak, miserable, and abject by refusing to lift their thoughts.

Before a person can achieve anything, even in worldly matters, they must raise their thoughts above base animal indulgence. To succeed, they may not need to give up all animality and selfishness, but they must at least sacrifice some of it. A person whose main focus is base indulgence cannot think clearly or plan methodically; they cannot find and develop their latent resources and will fail in any endeavor. Without beginning to control their thoughts, they are not ready to control affairs or take on serious responsibilities. They are not fit to act independently and stand alone. But they are limited only by the thoughts they choose.

There can be no progress, no achievement without sacrifice, and a person's worldly success will be proportional to how much they sacrifice their confused animal thoughts and focus their mind on developing their plans, strengthening their resolve, and becoming more self-reliant. The higher they lift their thoughts, the more manly, upright, and righteous they become, and the greater their success, the more blessed and enduring their achievements will be.

The universe does not favor the greedy, the dishonest, and the vicious, although it may sometimes appear to do so on the surface; it helps the honest, the generous, and the virtuous. All the great Teachers throughout history have declared this in various ways, and to prove and know it, a person has only to persist in making themselves more and more virtuous by raising their thoughts.

Intellectual achievements result from thought dedicated to the pursuit of knowledge or the beautiful and true in life and nature. Such achievements may sometimes be associated with vanity and ambition, but they are not caused by those traits; they naturally result from long and arduous effort and pure and unselfish thoughts.

Spiritual achievements are the culmination of holy aspirations. A person who constantly thinks noble and lofty thoughts and focuses on all that is pure and unselfish will, as surely as the sun reaches its peak and the moon becomes full, become wise and noble in character and rise to a position of influence and blessedness.

Achievement, of any kind, is the crown of effort and the diadem of thought. With self-control, resolution, purity, righteousness, and well-directed thought, a person rises; with animality, indolence, impurity, corruption, and confused thoughts, a person falls.

A person may rise to great success in the world and even reach high spiritual levels, but they can also fall back into weakness and misery by allowing arrogant, selfish, and corrupt thoughts to take over.

Victories achieved through right thinking can only be maintained with vigilance. Many people give up when success seems assured and quickly fall back into failure.

All achievements, whether in business, intellectual pursuits, or spiritual growth, result from well-directed thought, are governed by the same law, and follow the same method; the only difference is in the goal.

Someone who wants to achieve little must sacrifice little; someone who wants to achieve much must sacrifice much; someone who wants to reach great heights must make great sacrifices.

• • •

CHAPTER 6
VISIONS AND IDEALS

Dreamers are the saviors of the world. Just as the visible world is supported by the invisible, so people, through all their struggles, sins, and mundane tasks, are nourished by the beautiful visions of their solitary dreamers. Humanity cannot forget its dreamers or let their ideals fade away; it lives through them, recognizing them as the realities that it will one day see and know.

Composers, sculptors, painters, poets, prophets, sages—these are the creators of the future world, the architects of heaven. The world is beautiful because they have lived; without them, working humanity would perish.

Anyone who holds onto a beautiful vision, a lofty ideal in their heart, will one day realize it. Columbus had a vision of another world, and he discovered it. Copernicus imagined a universe full of worlds, and he revealed it. Buddha envisioned a spiritual world of pure beauty and perfect peace, and he entered it.

Cherish your visions; cherish your ideals; cherish the music that stirs in your heart, the beauty that forms in your mind, the loveliness that wraps around your purest thoughts. From them will grow all delightful conditions, all heavenly environments. If you stay true to them, your world will be built from them.

To desire is to obtain; to aspire is to achieve. Should man's basest desires be fully satisfied while his purest aspirations starve? This is not the Law: such a situation can never exist. "Ask and receive."

Dream big dreams, and as you dream, so shall you become. Your Vision is the promise of what you shall one day be; your Ideal is the prophecy of what you shall finally reveal.

The greatest achievement was once a dream. The oak sleeps in the acorn; the bird waits in the egg; and in the highest vision of the soul, an awakening angel stirs. Dreams are the seeds of reality.

Your circumstances may be unfavorable, but they will not remain so if you see an Ideal and strive to reach it. You cannot change within and remain unchanged without. Here is a young man struggling with poverty and labor; confined to long hours in an unhealthy workshop; uneducated and lacking refinement. But he dreams of better things: intelligence, refinement, grace, and beauty. He mentally builds an ideal life; the vision of greater freedom and opportunity fills him. Unrest drives him to action, and he uses his spare time and resources, however small, to develop his latent powers. Soon, his mind changes so much that the workshop can no longer contain him. It becomes so out of tune with his mentality that it falls away like an old garment, and as new opportunities match his expanding abilities, he leaves it forever. Years later, this young man becomes a mature leader. He masters certain mental forces, wielding worldwide influence and nearly unmatched power. He holds great responsibilities, speaks, and changes lives. People hang on his words and reshape their characters. He becomes the central, luminous figure around which countless destinies revolve. He has realized his youthful Vision. He has become one with his Ideal.

And you, young reader, will realize the Vision of your heart, whether it is base or beautiful, or a mix of both, because you will always gravitate towards what you secretly love most. You will receive the exact results of your thoughts; you will earn exactly what you deserve. Whatever your current environment, you will fall, remain, or rise with your thoughts, Vision, and Ideal. You will become as small as your strongest desire or as great as your highest aspiration. In the beautiful words of Stanton Kirkham Davis, "You may be keeping accounts, and soon you will walk out of the door that seemed to be the barrier to your ideals, and find yourself before an audience—the pen still behind your ear, the ink stains on your fingers, and there and then you will pour out the torrent of your inspiration. You may be driving sheep, and you will wander into the city, wide-eyed; you will follow the spirit into the master's studio, and after a while, he will say, 'I have nothing more to teach you.' Now you have become the master, who dreamed of great things while driving sheep. You will set down the saw and the plane to take on the regeneration of the world."

The thoughtless, ignorant, and lazy see only the apparent effects and not the things themselves. They talk of luck, fortune, and chance. Seeing someone grow rich, they say, "How lucky he is!" Observing someone become intellectual, they exclaim, "How fortunate he is!" Noticing the saintly character and influence of another, they remark, "How chance favors him!" They don't see the trials, failures, and struggles these people have voluntarily faced to gain their experience; they don't know the sacrifices made, the undaunted efforts, and the faith exercised to overcome the seemingly impossible and realize their heart's Vision. They don't know the darkness and heartaches; they only see the light and joy and call it "luck." They don't see the long, arduous journey but only the pleasant goal and call it "good fortune." They don't understand the process, only the result, and call it chance.

In all human affairs, there are efforts and results, and the strength of the effort measures the result. Chance does not exist. Gifts, powers, and material, intellectual, and spiritual possessions are the fruits of effort; they are thoughts completed, goals achieved, and visions realized.

The Vision you glorify in your mind, the Ideal you hold in your heart—this you will build your life upon; this you will become.

• • •

CHAPTER 7

SERENITY

Calmness of mind is one of the beautiful jewels of wisdom. It is the result of long and patient effort in self-control. Its presence indicates matured experience and a deeper knowledge of the laws and operations of thought.

A person becomes calm as they understand themselves as a being shaped by thought. This knowledge requires understanding others as being shaped by thought, too. As someone gains the right understanding and sees more clearly the connections of things through cause and effect, they stop fussing, fuming, worrying, and grieving, and instead remain poised, steadfast, and serene.

The calm person, having learned to control themselves, knows how to adapt to others. Others, in turn, respect their spiritual strength and feel they can learn from and rely on them. The more tranquil a person becomes, the greater their success, influence, and power for good. Even a regular businessperson will find their business prospering as they develop greater self-control and calmness, because people always prefer to deal with someone whose demeanor is steady and balanced.

The strong, calm person is always loved and respected. They are like a shade-giving tree in a thirsty land or a sheltering rock in a storm. Who doesn't love a calm heart and a sweet-tempered, balanced life? It doesn't matter whether it rains or shines, or what changes come to those with these blessings, for they are always sweet, serene, and calm. That exquisite balance of character, which we call serenity, is the final lesson of growth, the fruit of the soul. It is as precious as wisdom and more desirable than gold— yes, even fine gold. How insignificant mere money-seeking looks compared to a serene life— a life that lives in the ocean of Truth, beneath the waves, beyond the reach of tempests, in Eternal Calm!

How many people do we know who sour their lives, ruin all that is sweet and beautiful with explosive tempers, destroy their balance of character, and create bad blood! It is a question whether the majority of people do not ruin their lives and mar their happiness by lack of self-control. How few people do we meet in life who are well-balanced, who have that exquisite poise that is the hallmark of a developed character!

Yes, humanity surges with uncontrolled passion, is tumultuous with ungoverned grief, and is blown about by anxiety and doubt. Only the wise person, only one whose thoughts are controlled and purified, makes the winds and storms of the soul obey them.

Storm-tossed souls, wherever you may be, under whatever conditions you may live, know this: in the ocean of life, the isles of blessedness are smiling, and the sunny shore of your ideal awaits your arrival. Keep your hand firmly on the helm of thought. In the vessel of your soul lies the commanding Master; He only sleeps—awaken Him. Self-control is strength; right thought is mastery; calmness is power. Say to your heart, "Peace, be still!"

• • •

From Poverty to Power

James Allen

Foreword

I looked at the world and saw it was covered in sadness and burned by the harsh fires of suffering. I searched for the cause. I looked around but couldn't find it; I checked books, but it wasn't there either; then I looked inside myself and found both the cause and that I had made it myself. I looked even deeper and found the solution. I discovered one rule, the rule of Love; one life, which is living in harmony with that rule; one truth, the truth of a mind that has gained control and a heart that is calm and willing to follow. I dreamed of writing a book that could help men and women, whether rich or poor, educated or not, worldly or spiritual, to find within themselves the source of all success, all happiness, all achievements, and all truth. That dream stayed with me and eventually became real. Now, I send it out into the world with a mission of healing and blessing, knowing it will reach the homes and hearts of those who are waiting and ready to receive it.

James Allen

PART I

THE PATH TO PROSPERITY

1. The lesson of evil

Restlessness, pain, and sadness are part of life's shadows. There is no heart in the world that hasn't felt the sting of pain, no mind that hasn't been troubled, and no eye that hasn't shed tears of deep sorrow.

There is no home where disease and death, the great destroyers, haven't entered, tearing hearts apart and covering everything with sorrow. All people are caught in the strong web of evil, and pain, sadness, and hardship follow us all.

To escape or lessen this darkness, people often rush blindly into all sorts of paths, hoping to find lasting happiness.

Some turn to drinking or seek pleasure in unhealthy ways; others shut themselves away in luxury, trying to avoid the world's sorrows. Some chase after wealth or fame, making it their only goal, while others find comfort in religious rituals.

It may seem like they find happiness for a while, and their soul feels secure, forgetting about evil. But then sickness or some great sorrow, temptation, or misfortune suddenly comes, and the happiness they thought they had falls apart.

So, hanging over every joy is the threat of pain, ready to strike and shatter the soul that isn't protected by wisdom.

A child longs to grow up, while adults often wish for the carefree days of childhood. The poor feel trapped by poverty, and the rich often live in fear of becoming poor or spend their time chasing a fleeting happiness.

Sometimes, people feel they have found true peace and happiness in a certain religion, a philosophy, or by creating an artistic or intellectual ideal. But when a powerful temptation comes, they realize the religion isn't enough, the philosophy is useless, or the ideal they've spent years working on falls apart.

So, is there no way out of pain and sorrow? Is there no way to break free from evil? Is lasting happiness, peace, and success just a dream?

No, there is a way, and I speak of it with joy. There is a way to defeat evil forever; there is a process to overcome disease, poverty, and other hardships so they never return. There is a method to achieve lasting success without the fear of setbacks, and a practice to find unending peace and happiness.

The start of this path comes from gaining a true understanding of what evil is.

It's not enough to deny or ignore evil; you need to understand it. It's not enough to pray to God to take away the evil; you must learn why it exists and what lesson it holds for you.

It's pointless to be angry and frustrated about the chains that bind you; instead, you need to understand why and how you are bound. So, you must look beyond yourself and begin to examine and understand yourself.

You must stop being like a disobedient child in the school of life and start learning with humility and patience the lessons meant to guide you to perfection. For when evil is rightly understood, it is not an unstoppable force but a temporary phase of human experience, and it becomes a teacher to those willing to learn.

Evil isn't some force outside of you; it is an experience in your own heart. By carefully examining and correcting your heart, you will eventually discover the root of evil, and this will lead to its complete removal.

All evil is meant to correct or heal, so it isn't permanent. It is based in ignorance—ignorance of the true nature of things. As long as we remain in ignorance, we remain subject to evil.

There is no evil in the universe that isn't the result of ignorance, and if we are willing to learn from it, it will lead us to higher wisdom and then disappear. But people stay stuck in evil because they aren't willing or ready to learn the lesson it is trying to teach them.

I once knew a child who, every night, begged its mother to let it play with a candle. One night, when the mother wasn't looking, the child grabbed the candle and got burned. After that, the child never wanted to play with the candle again.

In that one act, the child learned the lesson of obedience perfectly and understood that fire burns. This is a perfect example of the nature, meaning, and ultimate result of all sin and evil.

Just as the child suffered from not knowing the true nature of fire, adults suffer from not knowing the true nature of the things they chase after, things that harm them when they finally get them. The only difference is that in adults, this ignorance and evil are deeper and harder to see.

Evil has always been symbolized by darkness, and good by light. Within this symbol is the perfect explanation: just as light fills the universe and darkness is only a shadow, so the Light of Good is the positive force that fills the universe, while evil is a tiny shadow cast by the self that blocks the light.

When night covers the world in darkness, no matter how dark it is, it only covers half of our little planet, while the entire universe is still filled with light. We all know that in the morning, the light will return.

In the same way, when the dark night of sorrow, pain, or trouble surrounds your soul, and you stumble forward unsure of your steps, remember that you are the one blocking the light of joy and peace. The shadow over you is cast by no one but yourself.

And just like the darkness outside is only a passing shadow, the darkness within you is also just a passing phase.

"But," you may ask, "why go through the darkness of evil at all?" Because, in ignorance, you have chosen to, and by doing so, you can understand both good and evil, and better appreciate the light by having passed through the darkness.

Since evil comes from ignorance, when we fully learn the lessons it offers, the ignorance fades away, and wisdom takes its place. But just like a disobedient child refuses to learn, people can also refuse to learn the lessons of life. By doing so, they stay in darkness and keep suffering through things like disease, disappointment, and sadness.

If you want to free yourself from the evil around you, you must be willing and ready to learn. You must be prepared to go through the process of discipline, because without it, you can't gain wisdom or lasting happiness and peace.

A person may lock themselves in a dark room and deny the existence of light, but the light is still everywhere outside, and the darkness only exists in their little room.

In the same way, you may shut out the light of truth, or you can begin tearing down the walls of selfishness and error that you've built around yourself, and let the ever-present Light shine in.

By examining yourself with honesty, strive to realize, not just as a theory, that evil is a temporary phase, a self-created shadow. Understand that all your pain, sorrow, and troubles have come to you by a perfect law. They have come because you deserve and need them, and by first accepting them and then understanding them, you will grow stronger, wiser, and better.

When you fully understand this, you will be able to shape your own circumstances, change all evil into good, and skillfully shape the path of your life.

> *What of the night, O Watchman! Do you see yet The faint*
> *dawn upon the mountain tops,*
> *The golden messenger of the Light of lights?*
> *Are his bright feet on the hilltops yet?*
> *Does he come to drive away the darkness, And with it*
> *all the demons of the night?*
> *Do his rays reach your sight?*
> *Do you hear his voice, announcing the end of error?*
> *The Morning comes, lover of the Light;*
> *Even now, it shines with gold on the mountain peaks.*
> *I see the path where his shining feet Are set to*
> *step toward the Night.*
> *Darkness will pass away,*
> *And all things that love the darkness and hate the Light Shall*
> *disappear forever with the night: Rejoice! The messenger*
> *of light sings.*

2. The world a reflex of mental states

What you are inside is what your world becomes. Everything in the universe reflects your inner experience. What's happening outside doesn't matter much because it's only a reflection of your thoughts and feelings.

What really matters is what's inside of you because everything around you will mirror that. Everything you truly know is part of your own experience; whatever you learn will come through experience and become part of who you are.

Your thoughts, desires, and goals create your world. To you, all the beauty and joy, or all the ugliness and sadness in the universe, is found within yourself.

Through your thoughts, you shape your life, your world, and your universe. As you build your inner world with the power of your thoughts, your outer life and circumstances will change to match it.

Whatever you keep deep in your heart will, sooner or later, shape your outer life according to the natural law of cause and effect.

A soul that is impure, selfish, and mean is headed toward misfortune and disaster. But a pure, unselfish, and noble soul is moving toward happiness and success.

Every soul attracts what belongs to it, and nothing can come to it that doesn't belong. Understanding this means recognizing the universal Law of the Divine.

The events in your life that help or harm you are brought about by the quality and strength of your inner thoughts. Every soul is a mix of its gathered thoughts and experiences, and the body is just a temporary vessel for the soul to express itself.

Your thoughts are your real self, and the world around you takes on the shape that your thoughts give it.

"All that we are is the result of what we have thought. It is based on our thoughts; it is made up of our thoughts," as Buddha said. This means that if someone is happy, it's because they focus on happy thoughts; if they are miserable, it's because they dwell on sad and weakening thoughts.

Whether someone is afraid or fearless, foolish or wise, troubled or peaceful, the cause of their state lies within them, never outside.

Now, I can almost hear someone asking, "Are you saying that outside events don't affect our minds?" I'm not saying that. What I'm saying, and what I know to be an unchanging truth, is that outside events can only affect you as much as you let them.

You're controlled by your circumstances because you don't fully understand the nature, power, and purpose of thought.

You believe (and it's this little word "belief" that holds all our joys and sorrows) that outside events can shape or ruin your life. By believing this, you submit to those outside events, confess that they are your master and you are their slave. By doing this, you give them a power they don't really have, and you fall, not to the events themselves, but to the feelings of gloom or happiness, fear or hope, strength or weakness, that your thoughts have placed around them.

I knew two men who, at a young age, lost all their hard-earned savings. One became very upset, letting worry and sadness take over.

The other, when reading the newspaper that his bank had failed and he lost everything, calmly said, "It's gone, and worry won't bring it back, but hard work will." He worked harder than before and soon became successful. Meanwhile, the first man, still mourning his loss and complaining about his "bad luck," remained stuck, trapped by his weak and negative thoughts.

The loss of money was a curse to the first man because he surrounded it with dark, hopeless thoughts. For the other, it was a blessing because he surrounded the event with thoughts of strength, hope, and renewed effort.

If circumstances had the power to bless or harm, they would affect all people the same way. But the fact that the same event can be good for one person and bad for another proves that the good or bad doesn't lie in the event, but in the mind of the person facing it.

When you begin to understand this, you'll start to control your thoughts, discipline your mind, and rebuild the inner world of your soul. You'll remove all unnecessary and harmful thoughts and fill yourself with thoughts of joy, peace, strength, life, kindness, love, beauty, and eternal life. As you do this, you will become joyful, peaceful, strong, healthy, kind, loving, and beautiful with the beauty of immortality.

Just as we surround events with our thoughts, we also surround the objects of the visible world with them. Where one person sees beauty and harmony, another sees ugliness.

One day, a passionate naturalist was exploring the countryside for fun and came across a pool of dirty water near a farmyard. While filling a small bottle with the water to study under a microscope, he excitedly told an uneducated farmer nearby about the countless wonders hidden in the pool. He said, "Yes, my friend, there are a hundred, no, a million universes in this pool if only we had the tools or the sense to see them." The farmer simply replied, "I know the water's full of tadpoles, but they're easy to catch."

Where the naturalist, full of knowledge, saw beauty, harmony, and hidden wonders, the farmer only saw a dirty mud puddle.

The wildflower that a passerby carelessly steps on is, to the poet, a messenger from the invisible world.

To many, the ocean is just a big, boring body of water where ships sometimes sink. But to the musician, it's alive, and they hear divine music in its changing moods. Where the average person sees chaos and disaster, the philosopher sees a perfect chain of cause and effect. Where the materialist sees only endless death, the mystic sees eternal, pulsing life.

Just as we surround events and objects with our thoughts, we also surround the souls of others with our thoughts.

The suspicious person believes everyone is suspicious. The liar feels safe believing no one else is honest. The envious see envy in everyone. The miser thinks everyone wants their money. The person who abandoned their conscience to make money sleeps with a gun under their pillow, thinking the world is full of people waiting to rob them. And the lustful person sees the saint as a hypocrite.

On the other hand, those who think loving thoughts find things to love everywhere. Honest and trusting people aren't worried about being lied to. The good-natured and generous, who celebrate the success of others, barely know what envy is. And those who have found the Divine within themselves recognize it in everyone, even animals.

Men and women are strengthened in their mental outlook because, by the law of cause and effect, they attract people who are like them.

The old saying, "Birds of a feather flock together," has a deeper meaning than people think. In the world of thoughts, as in the physical world, like attracts like.

Do you want kindness? Be kind. Do you seek truth? Be truthful. What you give of yourself, you will find. Your world is a reflection of you.

If you're one of those people who are hoping and praying for a happier world after death, here's a message of joy: You can experience that happy world now. It fills the entire universe, and it's inside you, waiting for you to find it, accept it, and make it yours. Someone who understood life's inner laws once said, "When people say, 'Look here, or look there,' don't go after them; the kingdom of God is within you."

All you need to do is believe this, believe it with a mind free of doubt, and then meditate on it until you fully understand it.

Then you'll start to purify and build your inner world. As you progress, moving from realization to realization, you will see the complete powerlessness of outer things compared to the amazing power of a soul that governs itself.

If you want to make the world right,
And get rid of all its evils and troubles,
Make the wild places bloom,
And make its empty deserts blossom like roses, Then
make yourself right.
If you want to free the world
From its long captivity in sin, Heal
all broken hearts,
And replace grief with sweet comfort,
Then change yourself.
If you want to heal the world
Of its long sickness, end its pain and sorrow,
Bring joy to everyone,
And give peace to the suffering,
Then heal yourself.
If you want to wake the world
From its dream of death and darkness,
Bring it to Love and Peace,
And the bright Light of eternal Life,
Then wake yourself.

3. The way out of undesirable conditions

After seeing and understanding that evil is just a passing shadow
caused by the self, blocking the view of the Eternal Good, and that
the world is a mirror showing each person a reflection of
themselves, we now rise, step by step, to the level of understanding
where we see the Law clearly.

With this understanding comes the realization that everything operates through an endless cycle of cause and effect, and nothing can exist outside of this law.

From the smallest thought, word, or action, to the movements of the stars, law rules everything. No random or arbitrary situation can exist, even for a moment, because that would mean the law could be broken, which is impossible.

Every situation in life follows an orderly, logical sequence, and the reason behind every condition is found within itself. The law, "Whatever a person sows, that they will also reap," is written in bold letters at the gateway of Eternity, and no one can deny it, avoid it, or escape it.

If someone touches fire, they will feel the burn, and neither anger nor prayers can change that.

This same law governs the mind. Hatred, anger, jealousy, envy, greed, and lust are like fires that burn, and anyone who engages with them must feel the pain.

These negative states of mind are called "evil" because they are the soul's way of trying to fight against the law, in ignorance. This leads to chaos and confusion inside and, sooner or later, shows up in life as sickness, failure, and misfortune, along with grief, pain, and despair.

On the other hand, love, kindness, goodwill, and purity are like cool breezes that bring peace to the soul. These are in harmony with the Eternal Law and show up in life as health, peaceful surroundings, and ongoing success and happiness.

A deep understanding of this Great Law that runs through the universe leads to a state of mind called obedience.

To know that justice, harmony, and love rule the universe is to know that all the negative and painful things in life are a result of our own disobedience to this Law.

Such knowledge brings strength and power, and it is only through this knowledge that a true life and lasting success and happiness can be built.

To remain patient in all situations and accept all conditions as necessary for your growth is to rise above all painful experiences and overcome them completely, without fear that they will return. This is because, through obedience to the law, they are completely defeated.

Someone who is obedient is working in harmony with the law and has, in fact, become one with the law. Whatever they conquer is conquered forever, and whatever they build can never be destroyed.

The source of all power, as well as all weakness, is within. The secret of all happiness, as well as all misery, is also within.

There is no progress without inner growth, and there can be no solid foundation for prosperity or peace without advancing in knowledge.

You may feel trapped by your circumstances. You might cry out for better opportunities, more freedom, or better living conditions, and maybe you curse the fate that holds you back.

I am writing this for you. I am speaking directly to you. Listen carefully, and let my words sink into your heart, because what I'm saying is true:

You can bring about the better conditions you desire in your life if you commit to improving your inner life.

I know this path looks difficult at first (truth often does; only error and illusion seem inviting and exciting at the start). But if you choose to walk this path, if you steadily discipline your mind, remove your weaknesses, and let your inner strength and spiritual power grow, you will be amazed at the changes that will happen in your outer life.

As you progress, opportunities will appear before you, and you will have the wisdom and ability to make the most of them. Good friends will come to you naturally, supportive souls will be drawn to you like a magnet, and books and other resources will come to you without effort.

Maybe you feel weighed down by poverty, or you are lonely and long for your burdens to be lifted, but the weight remains, and it feels like the darkness is growing. Maybe you complain about your situation, blame your birth, your parents, your boss, or an unfair universe for giving you poverty and hardship while others have wealth and comfort.

Stop complaining and worrying. None of these things are the cause of your poverty. The cause is within you, and where the cause is, the solution is too.

The fact that you are a complainer shows that you deserve your situation. It shows that you lack the faith that is the foundation of all effort and progress.

There is no place for a complainer in a universe governed by law, and worrying is like destroying your own soul. By thinking this way, you are making the chains that bind you stronger and creating the darkness that surrounds you.

Change your outlook on life, and your outer life will change too.

Build yourself up in faith and knowledge, and make yourself worthy of better surroundings and more opportunities. First, be sure that you are making the most of what you already have.

Don't fool yourself into thinking you can move on to greater things while ignoring the small things. If you did, those gains would be temporary, and you would soon fall back to learn the lesson you had skipped.

Just like a child in school must master one level before moving on to the next, you must faithfully use what you already have before you can receive the greater good you desire.

The parable of the talents beautifully illustrates this truth. It shows that if we misuse, neglect, or look down on what we have, no matter how little it may be, even that will be taken from us because our actions show we don't deserve it.

Maybe you live in a small house, surrounded by unhealthy or negative influences. You want a bigger, healthier home. Then you must first make yourself ready for such a home by turning your current house into a small paradise as much as possible. Keep it spotless. Make it as pretty and pleasant as your means allow. Cook your simple food with care, and set your humble table as nicely as you can.

If you can't afford a carpet, cover your floors with smiles and kindness, secured with the nails of kind words hammered in with patience. That kind of carpet won't fade in the sun, and constant use will never wear it out.

By making your current surroundings better, you will rise above them, and at the right time, you will move into a better home that has been waiting for you and that you are now ready to live in.

Maybe you want more time for thought and effort, but you feel like your hours of work are too long and hard. Then make sure you're using every bit of the spare time you have as effectively as possible.

It's useless to want more time if you're already wasting the time you have because you would just become more lazy and careless.

Even poverty and lack of time and leisure aren't as bad as you think. If they slow your progress, it's because you've surrounded them with your own weaknesses. The evil you see in them is really within yourself.

Try to fully understand that, as you shape and guide your mind, you are creating your own destiny. As you grow through self- discipline, you will see that these so- called evils can actually be turned into blessings.

You will use your poverty to grow patience, hope, and courage, and your lack of time to develop quick decision-making and prompt action, by seizing every moment as it comes.

Just as the most beautiful flowers grow in the richest soil, the finest human qualities develop and bloom in the soil of poverty.

Where there are difficulties to face and problems to solve, that's where virtue grows and shines the most.

Maybe you work for a cruel boss, and you feel you're being treated unfairly. See this too as part of your training. Return their unkindness with gentleness and forgiveness.

Practice patience and self-control without stopping. Turn the difficulty into an opportunity to build your mental and spiritual strength. By your quiet example, you will help your boss grow ashamed of their behavior, while at the same time, you will lift yourself to a higher spiritual level, allowing you to move into better, more fitting surroundings when the time comes.

Don't complain about being a slave. Instead, lift yourself up by noble behavior above the level of slavery. Before you complain about being a slave to someone else, be sure you aren't a slave to yourself.

Look within; search deeply, and don't let yourself off easy. You may find there are still slavish thoughts, slavish desires, and slavish habits in your daily life and behavior.

Conquer these. Stop being a slave to yourself, and no one will be able to enslave you. As you overcome yourself, you will overcome all difficult conditions, and every problem will fall before you.

Don't complain about being oppressed by the rich. Are you sure that if you became rich, you wouldn't become an oppressor yourself?

Remember that the Eternal Law is completely just. Those who oppress today will themselves be oppressed tomorrow. There is no escaping this.

And maybe, in a past life, you were rich and an oppressor, and now you're paying back the debt you owe to the Great Law. Practice patience and faith.

Keep your mind focused on Eternal justice and the Eternal Good. Try to rise above personal, temporary concerns and into the impersonal and everlasting.

Get rid of the idea that someone else is hurting or oppressing you, and try to understand, through a deeper awareness of your inner life and the laws that govern it, that the only thing that can hurt you is what's inside you.

There is no practice more damaging and soul-destroying than self-pity.

Get rid of it. As long as that disease is eating away at your heart, you can never expect to grow into a fuller life.

Stop criticizing others and start criticizing yourself. Don't excuse any of your actions, desires, or thoughts that can't stand up to perfect purity or the light of complete goodness.

By doing this, you will be building your life on the solid foundation of the Eternal, and everything you need for happiness and well-being will come to you in time.

There is no way to rise permanently above poverty or any unwanted condition without getting rid of the selfish and negative qualities inside you that those conditions reflect and continue to exist because of.

The way to true riches is to enrich your soul by growing in virtue. Outside of real heart-virtue, there is no prosperity or power, only the appearance of them. I know that people make money without gaining any virtue and without much desire for it. But that money is not true wealth, and its possession is temporary and restless. Here is David's testimony: "I was envious of the foolish when I saw the prosperity of the wicked... Their eyes bulged with fatness; they had more than their hearts could wish. I kept my heart clean for nothing, and washed my hands in innocence... When I tried to understand this, it was too painful for me, until I entered the sanctuary of God, then I understood their end."

The prosperity of the wicked was a great test for David until he entered the sanctuary of God, then he understood their fate.

You can enter that sanctuary too. It's inside you. It's the state of mind you reach when you rise above everything personal, temporary, and impure, and realize universal and eternal principles.

That is the God-consciousness, the sanctuary of the Most High. After you have struggled and practiced self-discipline to enter that holy place, you will be able to clearly see the outcome of all human thought and action, both good and evil.

You will no longer lose your faith when you see an immoral person getting rich because you will know that they will eventually return to poverty and suffering.

The rich person who has no virtue is really poor, and as surely as the river flows toward the ocean, they are drifting toward poverty and misfortune. Even if they die rich, they will still have to come back to reap the bitter fruit of their bad actions.

And no matter how many times they become rich, they will also fall back into poverty until, through experience and suffering, they finally conquer the poverty within.

But the person who is outwardly poor but rich in virtue is truly rich, and even in their poverty, they are on the path toward prosperity. Joy and happiness await them.

If you want to be truly and permanently prosperous, you must first become virtuous.

So, it is unwise to aim directly for prosperity or make it the main goal of life.

Reaching out greedily for it will only lead to failure.

Instead, aim for self-perfection. Make useful and unselfish service the goal of your life, and always reach out in faith to the supreme and unchanging Good.

You say you want wealth, not for yourself, but to help others and do good. If that is truly your motive, then wealth will come to you because you are strong and unselfish enough to see yourself as a steward, not an owner, in the midst of riches.

But take a close look at your real motive, because most of the time when people say they want money to help others, the real reason is that they like being popular or want to be seen as a good person or reformer.

If you're not helping others with the little you already have, then when you get more money, you'll likely become even more selfish. And any good you might try to do with your money would only serve to make you look better in the eyes of others. If you truly want to do good, you don't need to wait until you have more money; you can start right now, exactly where you are. If you are as unselfish as you think, you'll prove it by sacrificing your own needs for others today.

No matter how poor you are, there's always a way to give something of yourself, just like the widow who gave everything she had.

The heart that genuinely wants to help doesn't wait for money to start but goes forward and offers kindness and goodness to both friends and strangers alike.

Just as results come from actions, prosperity and power come from inner goodness, while poverty and weakness come from inner negativity.

Money is not true wealth, nor is status or power, and if you depend on them, you are building your life on shaky ground.

Your real wealth is the goodness inside you, and your real power is how you use that goodness.

Fix your heart, and you will fix your life. Lust, hatred, anger, pride, greed, selfishness, stubbornness—all these are forms of poverty and weakness. On the other hand, love, purity, kindness, humility, compassion, and generosity—all these are wealth and power.

As you overcome the things that make you weak, a strong and unstoppable power rises within you, and the person who masters the highest goodness will bring the world to their feet.

Both the rich and the poor have their struggles, and often, the rich are further from happiness than the poor. This shows us that happiness doesn't depend on things we own, but on how we live on the inside.

Maybe you're an employer, and you constantly struggle with your workers. Even when you find good employees, they leave quickly, and now you're losing faith in people.

You try to fix it by paying better wages or giving them more freedom, but nothing changes. Here's my advice:

The root of the problem isn't your workers, it's within you. If you search yourself honestly, with the desire to find and remove the problem, you'll eventually discover the source of your unhappiness.

It could be some selfish desire, suspicion, or unkind thought that affects those around you, even if you don't show it outwardly.

Think about your workers with kindness. Imagine doing the work you expect them to do and ask yourself if you would want to do it if you were in their place.

It's rare and admirable when a worker forgets themselves and focuses entirely on their employer's success. But even rarer, and even more beautiful, is the person who, forgetting their own happiness, seeks to make those under them happy and well-cared for.

A person like that finds their own happiness growing many times over and never has to complain about their employees. Asuccessful employer once said, "I've always had great relationships with my workers. If you ask me why, I'd say it's because I've always tried to treat them the way I'd want to be treated."

This is the key to creating good conditions and getting rid of bad ones.

Do you feel lonely, unloved, and without a single friend? If so, for your own happiness, stop blaming others and start with yourself.

Be friendly to others, and you'll soon find friends coming to you. Make yourself kind and lovable, and you will be loved by everyone.

Whatever is making your life difficult right now, you can rise above it by developing and using the power of self-purification and self-control within you.

Whether it's poverty that weighs you down (and I'm talking about the kind of poverty that causes misery, not the kind chosen by those who have found inner freedom), or the burden of wealth, or the misfortunes and annoyances that make life hard, you can overcome them by defeating the selfishness within that gives them power.

It doesn't matter if, by the unchanging Law, you must face the consequences of past actions, because at the same time, you're constantly setting new actions and thoughts into motion, and you have the power to make them good or bad.

And even if a person must lose money or status because of past choices, that doesn't mean they have to lose their strength or their honesty, because that's where true wealth, power, and happiness are found.

The person who holds onto selfishness is their own enemy, surrounded by troubles.

The person who lets go of selfishness is their own savior, surrounded by friends and blessings.

Before the light of a pure heart, all darkness fades, and all clouds disappear. The one who has conquered selfishness has conquered the world.

So, come out of your poverty, your pain, your struggles, your complaints, and your heartache by stepping out of yourself.

Let the worn-out clothing of your selfishness fall away, and put on the new garment of universal love.

Then, you will experience the heaven within, and it will show itself in your whole life.

The one who walks the path of self-mastery and carries the staff of Faith, walking the road of self-sacrifice, will surely find the greatest success and lasting joy.

> To those who seek the highest good,
> Everything works out for the best.
> Nothing happens by accident, and wisdom makes
> Even the worst things lead to something good.
> Sadness hides a star That's
> waiting to shine. Darkness
> turns to light, And after
> night,
> Comes golden glory from afar. Failures
> are steps that lead us higher, Towards
> better goals and nobler ends. Losses
> lead to gains, and joy follows The
> honest steps we take through life. Pain
> leads to paths of true happiness,

To thoughts and actions that are pure and kind.
And clouds that darken or rays that shine
Both kiss us as we move up life's road.
Misfortunes might cover the path
That rises up to the sky.
But at the end waits success,
Bright and kissed by the sun.
The heavy doubts and fears
That cloud the Valley of our dreams, The
struggles we face in spirit,
And the tears we shed,
The heartbreaks, sadness, and grief, And
the pain of broken ties,
These are all steps we climb To
reach true beliefs that last.
Love, watching with kindness,
Welcomes the traveler from the Land of Fate.
All glory and all goodness wait
For the feet that walk in faith.

4. The silent power of thought: controlling and directing one's forces

The strongest forces in the universe are the silent ones. The more powerful a force is, the more it becomes helpful when used correctly, and destructive when misused.

This is well understood when it comes to physical forces like steam or electricity, but few people apply this idea to the mind, where the most powerful forces of all— thoughts—are constantly being created and sent out as forces for either saving or harming.

At this stage of human development, we have control over these forces, and the whole direction of our progress is about learning to master them. All the wisdom we can gain in this world is found in complete self-control, and the command "Love your enemies" is an invitation to gain that wisdom by taking control of our thoughts, mastering them, and transforming them. Right now, most people are carried helplessly along by their selfish thoughts, like a straw floating on a stream.

The Hebrew prophets, with their deep understanding of the Supreme Law, always connected outward events to inner thoughts. They knew that national success or disaster came from the thoughts and desires that ruled the people at that time.

Their knowledge of the power of thought was the foundation of all their prophecies. National events are simply the results of a nation's collective thoughts.

Wars, plagues, and famines happen when people's thoughts clash and are wrongly directed. These destructive events are the consequences of wrong thinking.

It's foolish to blame wars on one person or a small group of people. Wars are the result of national selfishness. It's the silent, powerful thought-forces that bring everything into being.

The universe was created out of thought. Matter, in its most basic form, is just solidified thought. Everything people accomplish is first formed in thought and then made real.

Writers, inventors, and architects first create their works in their minds. Once they perfect it in thought, they begin to bring it into the physical world.

When thoughts are aligned with the higher laws of the universe, they build up and preserve. But when thoughts go against those laws, they break down and destroy.

If you align all your thoughts with faith in the power of Good, you will cooperate with that Good and see the solution to all evil within yourself. Believe, and you will truly live.

This is the true meaning of salvation—being saved from the darkness and negativity of evil by realizing and living in the light of Eternal Good.

Where there is fear, worry, doubt, or disappointment, there is ignorance and a lack of faith.

These states of mind are the direct results of selfishness and come from a deep belief in the power of evil. They are, in fact, a kind of atheism. To live in these negative, soul-destroying states of mind is the only real form of atheism.

What the world really needs is to be saved from these conditions, and no one should claim to be "saved" if they are still ruled by fear or worry.

To fear or worry is just as wrong as cursing, because how can anyone fear or worry if they truly believe in Eternal justice, All-powerful Good, and Infinite Love? To fear, worry, or doubt is to deny and disbelieve.

All weakness and failure come from these states of mind, because they cancel out the positive forces of thought that would otherwise bring good results.

Overcoming these negative conditions is the key to a life of power. It is the way to stop being a slave and start being a master. And the only way to do this is through steady and persistent growth in inner knowledge.

It's not enough to simply deny evil in your mind—you must rise above it through practice and understanding. It's not enough to just affirm the good—you must enter into it through consistent effort and fully understand it.

Practicing self-control leads quickly to a deeper knowledge of your inner thought-forces. Over time, it gives you the power to use and direct them correctly.

The more you control yourself and your mental forces, instead of letting them control you, the more you will have control over your circumstances and the events in your life.

Show me someone whose life keeps falling apart and who can't hold onto success, even when it's handed to them, and I'll show you someone who lives in constant doubt, fear, and anxiety.

To constantly sink in doubt, to be pulled into the quicksand of fear, or to be tossed around by the winds of worry, is to live like a slave, even if success and influence are always knocking at your door, trying to come in.

A person without faith or self-control can't manage their affairs correctly and becomes a slave to circumstances—ultimately, a slave to themselves. These people often learn through hardship, and eventually, they grow stronger through painful experiences.

Faith and purpose are the driving forces of life.

There is nothing that strong faith and a firm purpose cannot accomplish. By daily practicing quiet faith, your thought-forces are gathered together. And by daily strengthening your purpose, those forces are directed toward your goals.

Whatever your position in life, before you can achieve any level of success, usefulness, or power, you must learn how to focus your thought-forces by cultivating calmness and peace.

Let's say you're a businessperson, and suddenly you face a huge problem or possible disaster. You become fearful and anxious, and don't know what to do.

If you stay in this state of mind, it will be disastrous because when fear takes over, good judgment disappears. But if you find a quiet hour in the early morning or at night and go to a place where you won't be disturbed, you can calm your mind. Sit in a relaxed position and think about something in your life that brings you peace and happiness. Gradually, a calm strength will come over you, and your anxiety will fade away.

When your mind starts to go back to worrying, bring it back to a place of peace and strength.

Once your mind is fully calm, you can focus all your attention on solving the problem. What seemed impossible to fix when you were anxious will now become clear and easy, and you will know exactly what to do with the perfect judgment that comes from a calm mind.

You may have to try day after day to calm your mind, but if you keep at it, you will succeed. And when you are calm and clear, the solution that comes to you must be followed.

When you return to the business of the day and the worries start creeping back in, you may start to doubt your solution. But don't listen to those doubts.

Trust completely in the vision that came during your moment of calm, not in the shadows of your anxiety. The time of calm is the time of clarity and correct judgment.

By practicing this mental discipline, you gather your scattered thoughts and focus them like a searchlight on the problem, and the problem will disappear before that focused power.

There is no difficulty, no matter how big, that can stand up to a calm and concentrated mind. And there is no goal that can't be quickly achieved with the intelligent use of your soul's power.

Until you have looked deeply within yourself and overcome many inner enemies, you won't fully understand the power of thought or how it connects to the material world. But when your thoughts are balanced and directed correctly, they can change your life in amazing ways.

Every thought you think is a force you send out. It will find a place in the minds of those who are open to it and will come back to you, bringing either good or bad. There is constant give-and- take between minds, and an endless exchange of thought- forces.

Selfish and harmful thoughts are destructive forces, like messengers of evil sent out to stir up negativity in other minds, which then send that negativity back to you, even stronger.

But thoughts that are calm, pure, and unselfish are like angels sent out into the world, carrying health, healing, and blessings. They counteract the evil forces, pour joy into troubled hearts, and restore broken spirits to their natural state of peace and life.

Think good thoughts, and they will soon show up in your life as good conditions. Control your soul's forces, and you will be able to shape your life however you want.

The difference between a savior and a sinner is that the savior has complete control over their inner forces, while the sinner is controlled by them.

There is no other way to true power and lasting peace except through self- control, self-government, and self-purification. To be ruled by your emotions is to be powerless, unhappy, and of little real help in the world.

The task before you is to conquer your moods, your shifting likes and dislikes, your sudden bursts of anger, suspicion, and jealousy—all the emotional changes you feel powerless against. Only then will you be able to weave the golden threads of happiness and prosperity into the fabric of your life.

As long as you are controlled by these changing moods, you will need to rely on others and on outside help to get through life.

If you want to walk confidently, achieve your goals, and succeed in life, you must learn to rise above and control all these disturbing and distracting feelings.

You must practice calming your mind every day, taking time to "go into the silence," as it's often called. This is the process of replacing a troubled thought with one of peace, replacing a thought of weakness with one of strength.

Until you can do this, you can't expect to direct your mental forces toward solving life's problems with any real success. It's about gathering your scattered forces and focusing them in one strong direction.

Just as draining and redirecting the streams of a marsh can turn it into a field of golden corn, mastering and focusing your thoughts can transform your heart and life.

As you gain control over your impulses and thoughts, you will start to feel a new, quiet power growing within you, and a sense of calm strength will stay with you.

Your hidden abilities will begin to unfold, and while before your efforts were weak and unsuccessful, you will now be able to work with a calm confidence that leads to success.

Along with this new strength, your inner vision—your intuition—will begin to awaken, and you will no longer walk in confusion but in light and certainty.

As this soul-vision develops, your ability to judge situations and understand them clearly will grow, and you will gain a sense of what is coming and the likely outcomes of your efforts.

As you change from within, your view of life will also change, and as you change your attitude toward others, their attitude and behavior toward you will also change.

As you rise above the lower, weakening thought-forces, you will connect with the positive, strengthening forces of strong, pure minds. Your happiness will grow beyond what you imagined, and you will begin to experience the joy, strength, and power that only come from self-mastery.

This joy, strength, and power will radiate from you. Without even trying, and often without knowing it, you will draw strong people to you. Influence will naturally come into your hands, and as your thought-world changes, the events in your life will change as well.

"A man's enemies are those of his own household." If you want to be useful, strong, and happy, you must stop letting negative, harmful thoughts run your mind. Just as a wise person controls their home and chooses their guests, so must you control your desires and decide which thoughts you allow into the home of your soul.

Even small steps toward self-mastery will greatly increase your power. But the person who perfects this divine skill will gain wisdom, inner strength, and peace beyond imagination. They will find that all the forces of the universe support and protect them as the master of their soul.

Do you want to reach the highest heaven? Do
you want to escape the lowest hell?
Live in thoughts of beauty,
Or dwell in thoughts of darkness.
For your thoughts are heaven above you, And
your thoughts are hell below.
Joy comes from good thoughts, And
pain comes from bad thoughts.
Worlds exist because of thoughts;
Glory comes from dreams.
And the story of time itself Flows
from the Eternal Thought.
Dignity, shame, sorrow, pain, and love
Are just masks for the mighty
Pulsing Thought that rules fate. As
the colors of the rainbow Come
from one colorless light, So the
changes in life
Come from one Eternal Dream.
And that dream is inside you,
Waiting for the dawn
That will wake it up
Into the living, strong thought
That will turn your ideal into reality,
Erase the nightmares of hell,
And lead you to the highest heaven,
Where the pure and perfect live.
Evil is just a thought that sees it;
Good is the thought that creates it.
Light, darkness, sin, and purity All
come from the way we think.

Dwell on the greatest thought,
And the greatest you will see.
Fix your mind on the Highest,
And the Highest you will be.

5. The secret of health, success and power

We all remember how much we loved hearing fairy tales when we were children. We eagerly followed the adventures of the good boy or girl, who were always protected at the last minute from the evil plans of the wicked witch, the cruel giant, or the bad king.

Our little hearts never worried about the hero or heroine, and we never doubted that they would win in the end, because we believed that the fairies were perfect and would never abandon those who were good and true.

What joy we felt when the Fairy-Queen, using all her magic at just the right moment, would get rid of all the darkness and trouble, and make sure the heroes' dreams came true so they could live "happily ever after."

As we grew older and became more familiar with what we call the "realities" of life, our beautiful fairy-world faded away, and we pushed its amazing characters into the shadows of our memory, thinking they were no longer real.

We believed we were wise and strong for leaving behind our childhood dreams, but when we become wise again—like little children—we'll return to those dreams and realize they are true after all.

The fairies, who are small and almost always invisible but hold great magical power, will come back to life in the soul of the person who grows in wisdom and understands the power of thought and the laws that govern our inner world.

To that person, the fairies will live again as thoughts, as messengers, as forces of the mind working in harmony with the greater Good. Those who work every day to align their hearts with the Supreme Good will truly find health, wealth, and happiness.

There is no greater protection than goodness. And by "goodness," I don't just mean following the rules of morality. I mean having pure thoughts, noble goals, unselfish love, and freedom from pride.

To live in good thoughts all the time is to create a kind and powerful energy around yourself, which will affect everyone you meet.

Just like the rising sun drives away the shadows, the forces of evil are powerless against the bright, positive energy that comes from a heart full of purity and faith.

Where there is strong faith and uncompromising purity, there is health, success, and power. In a person like this, disease, failure, and disaster can't find a place to exist because there's nothing for them to feed on.

Even our physical health is influenced by our mental state, and science is quickly recognizing this truth.

The old belief that a person is the way they are because of their body is fading away. It's being replaced by the inspiring idea that a person is greater than their body, and that the body becomes what we make it through the power of thought.

People are starting to realize that it's not that a person is sad because they have stomach problems; it's that they have stomach problems because they are sad. And soon, the fact that all disease starts in the mind will be common knowledge.

There is no evil in the universe that doesn't start in the mind. Sin, sickness, sorrow, and suffering don't belong to the natural order of the universe. They come from our misunderstanding of how things truly relate to each other.

According to an old story, there once lived a group of philosophers in India who lived such pure and simple lives that they often lived to be 150 years old. Getting sick was seen as a great shame because it was thought to be a sign that they had broken the laws of life.

The sooner we realize that sickness is not a punishment from God or a test from the universe, but the result of our own mistakes or wrong thoughts, the sooner we will find the path to health.

Disease comes to those who invite it with their thoughts and actions. It avoids those whose strong, pure, and positive minds create healing and life-giving energy.

If you are full of anger, worry, jealousy, greed, or any other negative state of mind, but still expect to have perfect health, you are asking for the impossible. You are constantly planting the seeds of disease in your mind.

A wise person avoids these negative states because they know that they are more dangerous than a bad drain or an unhealthy environment.

If you want to be free from all physical aches and pains and have perfect physical health, you must first put your mind in order and harmonize your thoughts. Think joyful thoughts. Think loving thoughts. Let the healing energy of goodwill flow through you, and you won't need any other medicine. Let go of your jealousies, suspicions, worries, hatreds, and selfish desires, and you will let go of your stomach problems, bad digestion, nervousness, and aching joints.

If you insist on holding onto these draining and harmful mental habits, then don't complain when your body gets sick. The following story shows how closely connected the mind and body are.

A man was suffering from a painful disease. He went to many different doctors, but none of them could help him. He traveled to towns famous for their healing waters, but after trying them all, his disease only got worse.

One night, he dreamed that a Presence came to him and said, "Brother, have you tried every cure?" The man replied, "I have tried everything." The Presence said, "No, come with me, and I will show you a healing bath you haven't tried yet."

The man followed the Presence, who led him to a clear pool of water and said, "Plunge into this water, and you will be healed." Then the Presence disappeared.

The man jumped into the water, and when he came out, his disease was gone. At the same moment, he saw the word "Renounce" written above the pool. When he woke up, the meaning of his dream became clear to him. He realized he had been a slave to a bad habit, and he promised to give it up forever.

He kept his promise, and from that day, his disease began to fade away. Soon, he was completely healthy.

Many people complain that they have become sick from overworking. In most cases, the sickness is more often caused by wasted energy, not by work.

If you want to stay healthy, you must learn how to work without stress. Becoming anxious or upset, or worrying about little details, is an invitation to illness. Work, whether physical or mental, is good for you and brings health. The person who can work calmly and steadily, without anxiety or worry, and with their mind focused only on the task at hand, will not only achieve more than the person who is always rushed and stressed, but they will keep their health, which the other person will lose.

True health and true success go together because they are deeply connected in the mind. Just as mental harmony creates physical health, it also leads to a smooth and successful life.

If you order your thoughts, you will order your life. Pour the calm oil of peace over the stormy waters of your emotions and prejudices, and the storms of misfortune, no matter how threatening, will not be able to sink the ship of your soul as it sails across the sea of life.

And if that ship is guided by a cheerful and steady faith, its journey will be even more certain, and many dangers that might have attacked it will pass by harmlessly. By the power of faith, every lasting work is accomplished. Faith in the Supreme Power, faith in the laws of the universe, faith in your work, and faith in your ability to complete it—this is the foundation you must build on if you want to succeed and stand strong.

Follow, in every situation, the highest voice within you. Always stay true to your best self. Trust in the inner Light, the inner Voice, and pursue your goals with a fearless and peaceful heart, believing that your future will bring you the results of every good thought and action. Know that the laws of the universe never fail and that what you give will come back to you with perfect accuracy. This is faith and living by faith.

By the power of this kind of faith, the dark waters of uncertainty will part, every mountain of difficulty will crumble, and the faithful soul will pass through unharmed.

Work, dear reader, to develop this priceless faith above all else. It is the key to happiness, success, peace, and power—everything that makes life great and lifts it above suffering.

Build your life on this faith, and you will build on the Rock of Eternity, using materials that last forever. The structure you create will never fall apart because it will rise above the temporary pleasures and riches of this world, which eventually turn to dust.

Whether you are thrown into the depths of sorrow or lifted to the heights of joy, always hold onto this faith. Always return to it as your refuge and keep your feet firmly planted on its unshakable foundation.

With this faith at your center, you will gain a spiritual strength that will smash, like fragile glass toys, all the forces of evil thrown against you. You will achieve a success that those who chase after worldly wealth can never understand or even imagine. "If you have faith and do not doubt, you will not only do what was done to the fig tree, but even if you say to this mountain, 'Be removed and thrown into the sea,' it will be done."

There are people today, living in flesh and blood, who have realized this kind of faith. They live by it every day, and after testing it to the fullest, they have entered into its peace and glory.

These people have given commands, and the mountains of sorrow, disappointment, mental exhaustion, and physical pain have been removed and thrown into the sea of forgetfulness.

If you develop this faith, you won't need to worry about success or failure— success will come naturally.

You won't need to be anxious about results. You will work joyfully and peacefully, knowing that right thoughts and right efforts will always bring about the right outcomes.

I know a woman who has experienced many blessings, and a friend recently said to her, "Oh, how lucky you are! It seems like whatever you wish for just happens."

On the surface, it did seem that way. But in truth, all the good things that have come into her life are the direct result of the inner peace and blessedness that she has spent her whole life developing and perfecting.

Simply wishing for things doesn't bring results—it's the way you live that makes the difference.

Foolish people wish and complain. Wise people work and wait. This woman had worked—both inside and out, but especially within, on her heart and soul. With the invisible hands of her spirit, she built up, using the precious stones of faith, hope, joy, dedication, and love, a beautiful temple of light. Its radiant glow surrounded her everywhere she went.

It shone in her eyes, brightened her face, and vibrated in her voice. Everyone who met her felt its magic.

And just as she did, so can you. Your success or failure, your influence, and your entire life are shaped by the thoughts you carry with you. Your dominant thoughts are the main factors that determine your future.

Send out loving, pure, and happy thoughts, and blessings will come to you, and your life will be filled with peace.

Send out hateful, impure, and unhappy thoughts, and curses will come to you, and fear and worry will fill your nights. You are the one who creates your own future, whatever that may be. Every moment, you are sending out the energy that will either make or break your life.

Let your heart grow large, loving, and unselfish, and your influence and success will be great and lasting, even if you don't make much money.

But if you focus only on yourself, then even if you become a millionaire, your influence and success will be meaningless in the end.

So, cultivate a pure and unselfish spirit. Combine this with faith and a clear purpose, and you will be developing not only great health and lasting success but also true greatness and power.

If your current job is unpleasant or you're not passionate about it, still perform your duties carefully. At the same time, keep in mind that better opportunities are waiting for you, and always be alert for new possibilities. When the right opportunity comes, you'll be ready to step into it with a well-prepared mind, using the wisdom and foresight that come from mental discipline.

Whatever your job is, focus all your attention on it and put all your energy into it. Doing small tasks perfectly will naturally lead to bigger opportunities. Climb steadily, and you'll never fall. This is the secret of true power.

Learn, through constant practice, how to save your energy and focus it on one goal at a time. Foolish people waste all their mental and spiritual energy on trivial things, silly conversations, or pointless arguments—not to mention harmful physical excesses.

If you want to gain the power to overcome, you must develop calmness and control. You must learn to stand strong on your own. All power comes from being steady and unmovable. The mountain, the huge rock, and the strong oak tree that survives storms all show power because they stand alone with strength and don't move. On the other hand, the shifting sand, the bending twig, and the swaying reed show weakness because they are movable and useless when separated from others.

A person who stays calm and unmoved when everyone around them is caught up in emotion or passion is a person of power. Only someone who has learned to control themselves is ready to lead and control others.

Those who are emotional, fearful, thoughtless, or shallow will need to rely on others for support, or they will fall. But those who are calm, fearless, and thoughtful should seek solitude in nature, like in the forest, the desert, or on a mountain. This will make them even stronger, and they will be able to resist the powerful emotional forces that overwhelm most people.

Passion is not power; it is the misuse of power. Passion is like a wild storm that beats against the strong rock, while true power is like the rock itself, remaining calm and still no matter what.

We see an example of true power in Martin Luther, when his fearful friends warned him not to go to Worms because of the danger. He replied, "If there were as many devils in Worms as there are tiles on the rooftops, I would still go."

Another example is Benjamin Disraeli, who failed in his first speech to Parliament and was laughed at by the crowd. He showed the beginnings of real power when he said, "The day will come when you will be honored to listen to me." I once knew a young man who faced constant setbacks and failures. His friends made fun of him and told him to give up, but he replied, "It won't be long before you'll be amazed at my good fortune and success." He showed that quiet, unstoppable power that eventually helped him overcome many difficulties and achieve success.

If you don't have this power yet, you can develop it through practice, and the beginning of power is also the beginning of wisdom. You must start by stopping the small, meaningless habits that you've been allowing to control you.

Excessive, uncontrolled laughter, gossiping, and joking just to make people laugh—these are wastes of valuable energy that you need to let go of.

The apostle Paul showed great insight into human progress when he warned the Ephesians against "foolish talk and jokes that are inappropriate," because to engage in these things regularly is to destroy your spiritual power.

As you become less affected by these distractions, you'll begin to understand what true power really is. Then, you can start to overcome the bigger desires and cravings that hold your soul back and block your path to power. With this, your way forward will become clearer.

Above all, be focused. Have a clear and useful purpose, and dedicate yourself fully to it. Don't let anything distract you. Remember, a person who can't stay focused is unstable in everything they do.

Be eager to learn, but don't beg for help. Know your work well, and make sure it's truly your own. As you move forward, following your inner guide and listening to the infallible voice inside you, you will achieve victory after victory. With each step, your view of life will expand, and you will gradually see the true beauty and purpose of life.

If you purify yourself, you will have health. If you protect yourself with faith, success will follow. If you govern yourself, you will have power, and everything you do will prosper. You will no longer be a confused, enslaved individual but will be in harmony with the great laws of the universe, working with the eternal Good instead of against it.

The health you gain will last. The success you achieve will be beyond what anyone can measure, and it will never fade. The influence and power you have will continue to grow over time, because they will be part of the unchangeable principle that holds up the universe.

This, then, is the secret of health—a pure heart and a well-ordered mind. This is the secret of success—an unwavering faith and a wisely directed purpose. And to control, with a steady will, the strong force of desire—this is the secret of power.

All paths are open for me to walk—
The light and dark, the living and the dead,
The wide and narrow, the high and low, The
good and bad, with quick steps or slow. I may
choose any path I want,
And by walking it,
I'll learn what's good or bad.
And all good things are waiting for me If
I come with an unbreakable promise
To stay on the narrow, high, and holy path Of
purity born from the heart.
Then I will walk, safe from those who mock, Through
meadows of flowers, across paths of thorns. I may
stand where health, success, and power
Wait for me, if, each passing hour, I
hold on to love and patience, Stay
pure, and never step away From
integrity.
Then I will see, at last, the land of eternal life.
I may search and find,
I may achieve.
I may lose, but I can also recover.
The law doesn't bend for me,
But I must bend to the law
If I want to end my suffering,
If I want to restore my soul
To light and life, and weep no more. It
is not my place to demand
All good things for myself.
Let my goal be to search, find, know, and understand,
And walk with holy footsteps toward wisdom.

I cannot claim or command anything,
But I can seek to know and understand everything.

6. The secret of abounding happiness

People have a deep desire for happiness, but most people lack it. Many poor people think that becoming rich will bring them lasting happiness. But there are many rich people who, after fulfilling every desire and wish, feel bored and empty. In fact, they are often farther from happiness than the poor.

If we think carefully about this, we'll come to realize an important truth: happiness doesn't come from having things, and misery doesn't come from lacking them. If that were true, all poor people would always be unhappy, and all rich people would always be happy. But the opposite is often true.

Some of the saddest people I've met were surrounded by riches and luxury, while some of the happiest people I've known had only the bare necessities of life.

Many wealthy people have admitted that the selfish enjoyment that comes with riches has taken the sweetness out of life. They say they were never as happy as when they were poor.

So, what is happiness, and how do we find it? Is it just an illusion? Is suffering all there is in life? After careful observation, we'll find that most people, except those who have gained wisdom, believe that happiness comes from fulfilling their desires.

This belief, rooted in ignorance and fed by selfish cravings, is the cause of all the misery in the world.

And I'm not just talking about basic physical desires. Even in the higher realms of the mind, more powerful, subtle, and tricky cravings keep even the most educated and refined people trapped, stopping them from experiencing the beauty, harmony, and purity of soul that lead to happiness.

Most people will admit that selfishness causes unhappiness, but they make the mistake of thinking that it's someone else's selfishness, not their own.

When you are ready to admit that all your unhappiness comes from your own selfishness, you'll be close to finding happiness. But as long as you blame others for robbing you of joy, you will stay trapped in a miserable situation you created for yourself.

Happiness is an inner state of perfect satisfaction, which brings joy and peace. In this state, all desire is gone. The happiness that comes from getting what we want is brief and misleading. It's always followed by an even greater desire for more.

Desire is like the ocean—it's never satisfied and demands more and more as we give in to it. It constantly asks for more attention from those who are fooled by it, until it finally overwhelms them with physical or mental pain and throws them into the cleansing fires of suffering. Desire is the source of hell, and all torments come from it.

Letting go of desire is how we enter heaven, and all joys are waiting there for those who give up selfish craving.

"I sent my soul out to learn about life after death,

And when it returned, it whispered, 'I am both heaven and hell.'"

Heaven and hell are states of mind. When you focus on yourself and your desires, you sink into hell. When you rise above yourself into a state where you forget about your own needs, you enter heaven.

The self is blind, lacks good judgment, and has no true knowledge. It always leads to suffering. Clear perception, good judgment, and true knowledge come only from the divine state of mind. The more you connect with this divine consciousness, the more you'll know what real happiness is.

As long as you keep selfishly chasing after your own personal happiness, it will slip away from you, and you'll be planting seeds of misery.

But as you succeed in losing yourself in service to others, happiness will come to you, and you will reap a harvest of joy. It

is in loving, not in being loved, That the heart is blessed.

It is in giving, not in receiving,

That we find what we're looking for.

Whatever you long for or need, Give it to others.

Then your soul will be fed, And you will truly live.

Hold on to yourself, and you hold on to sorrow. Let go of yourself, and you enter peace. Chasing after happiness for selfish reasons will not only make you lose happiness, but it will also make you lose what you think brings happiness.

Look at the glutton, who is always searching for the next tasty food to excite his dulled appetite. In the end, he becomes so full, bloated, and sick that hardly any food brings him joy.

On the other hand, the person who controls their appetite and doesn't even think about the pleasure of eating enjoys even the simplest meal.

The happiness that people think they see in fulfilling desires turns out to be the skeleton of misery when they finally grasp it. Truly, "He who tries to save his life will lose it, but he who gives up his life will find it."

Lasting happiness will come to you when you stop holding on and are willing to let go. When you're ready to give up that temporary thing that is so dear to you— something that will be taken from you one day whether you like it or not—you will find that what seemed like a painful loss turns out to be a great gain.

Giving up to gain something is one of the biggest illusions and a major cause of misery. But being willing to give up and accept loss is the real path to life.

How can we find real happiness by clinging to things that are temporary and must pass away? True, lasting happiness can only be found by focusing on what is permanent.

Rise above the need for temporary things, and you will enter a consciousness of the Eternal. As you rise above yourself and grow into a spirit of purity, self-sacrifice, and universal love, you will find the happiness that has no downside and can never be taken from you.

The heart that has completely forgotten itself in love for others has not only found the highest happiness but has also touched immortality because it has realized the Divine.

Look back at your life, and you'll see that the moments of greatest happiness were the times when you spoke a kind word or performed an act of selfless love. Spiritually, happiness and harmony are the same.

Harmony is a part of the Great Law, and its spiritual expression is love. All selfishness is discord, and to be selfish is to go against the divine order.

As we realize the love that denies the self, we put ourselves in harmony with the divine music of the universe, and that beautiful melody, which is true happiness, becomes our own.

Men and women are running here and there, blindly searching for happiness but never finding it. They will never find it until they realize that happiness is already inside them and all around them, filling the universe. By selfishly searching for it, they are shutting themselves off from it.

> I chased happiness, trying to make it mine,
> Through towering oaks and hanging ivy vines. I
> chased it over hills and valleys,
> Over fields and meadows in the purple light. I
> crossed rivers and climbed steep cliffs,

But happiness always slipped away.
Exhausted, I gave up, sinking to rest
On a lonely shore.
One person came asking for food,
Another for help.
I gave bread and gold to each,
And shared my heart with all who came.
Then, suddenly, happiness,
In its divine form, stood beside me,
Whispering, "I am yours."

These beautiful words by Burleigh show the secret to happiness. Let go of the personal and temporary, and you'll rise into the eternal. Give up the small self that tries to control everything for its own gain, and you'll find yourself in the company of angels, in the heart of universal love.

Forget yourself completely in helping others, and divine happiness will free you from all suffering.

"Taking the first step with a kind thought, The second with a kind word,

And the third with a kind act, I entered Paradise."

You can enter Paradise by following this same path. It's not far away—it's here. It can only be known by the unselfish and is fully realized only by those pure in heart.

If you haven't yet found this boundless happiness, you can begin to discover it by always aiming for the ideal of unselfish love and striving toward it.

Aspiration, or prayer, is desire turned upward. It is the soul reaching out to its divine source, where true satisfaction can be found. Through aspiration, the harmful forces of desire are transformed into divine, life-giving energy.

To aspire is to try to shake off the chains of desire. It's like the lost son, who, after learning from loneliness and suffering, returns to his father's house.

As you rise above selfishness and break the chains that bind you, you will experience the joy of giving, which is very different from the misery of selfishly taking. You will then understand that it is truly "more blessed to give than to receive."

But this giving must come from the heart, without any trace of selfishness or expectation of reward. The gift of pure love always brings joy.

If, after giving, you feel hurt because you weren't thanked or praised, or your name wasn't mentioned, know that your gift was given out of vanity, not love. You weren't really giving; you were trying to take.

Lose yourself in the welfare of others. Forget yourself in everything you do.

This is the secret of true and lasting happiness.

Always be on guard against selfishness and learn the divine lessons of inner sacrifice. This way, you will climb to the highest levels of happiness and remain in the endless sunshine of universal joy, wrapped in the shining garment of immortality.

Are you searching for the happiness that never fades?
Are you looking for the joy that lasts and never brings
sorrow?
Are you longing for the refreshing waters of Love, Life, and
Peace?
Then let all dark desires go, and stop selfish seeking.
Are you wandering down paths of pain,
Haunted by grief and hurt?
Are you walking the roads that make your feet more tired? Are
you sighing for the resting place where tears and sorrows end?
Then sacrifice your selfish heart, and find the Heart of
Peace.

7. The realization of prosperity

Only a heart full of honesty, trust, generosity, and love can
experience true prosperity. If you don't have these qualities, you
can't know prosperity, because prosperity—like happiness—isn't
something you can own, it's something you feel inside.

A greedy person may become rich, but they will always feel
miserable, mean, and poor. They will even see themselves as poor if
there's someone richer than them. On the other hand, a person who
is honest, generous, and loving will feel truly prosperous, even if
they don't have much.

A person is poor if they are always unsatisfied. A person is rich if they
are happy with what they have. And someone is even richer if they
are willing to share what they have.

When we think about the fact that the universe is filled with all kinds of good things—both material and spiritual—and compare that to people's blind desire to grab a few gold coins or a little bit of land, we can see how dark and ignorant selfishness is. We then understand that selfishness leads to destruction.

Nature gives everything freely and loses nothing, but people who try to grab everything end up losing it all.

If you want to experience true prosperity, don't fall into the trap of believing that doing the right thing will make everything go wrong. Don't let the word "competition" shake your belief in the power of doing what's right.

I don't care what people say about the "laws of competition," because I know the unchangeable law that will eventually prove them wrong. In fact, it's already proving them wrong in the heart and life of any honest person.

Knowing this law allows me to look at dishonesty without being disturbed because I know that destruction is waiting for it. No matter what, always do what you believe is right, and trust the law. Trust the divine power that runs through the universe, and it will never let you down—you will always be protected.

By having this kind of trust, any loss will turn into a gain, and any curse will turn into a blessing. Never let go of integrity, generosity, and love. Combined with hard work, these will lift you into a truly prosperous life.

Don't listen to the world when it tells you to take care of yourself first and think of others later. Living this way means you're not really thinking about others at all— only your own comfort.

People who live this way will eventually find themselves alone. When they cry out for help in their loneliness and pain, there will be no one to hear them. Putting yourself first stops every noble and good impulse.

Let your heart expand. Reach out to others with love and generosity, and you will experience great and lasting joy, and prosperity will follow.

People who leave the path of doing what's right always worry about competition. But those who stay on the path of righteousness don't need to worry about competition.

This isn't just a nice saying. There are people today who, by being honest and faithful, have beaten all competition. Even when others tried to undermine them, these honest people stayed true to their values and steadily rose to prosperity, while those who tried to bring them down failed.

Having the qualities of goodness in your heart protects you from all the forces of evil. It strengthens you in every time of trouble. Building yourself up in these qualities leads to success that cannot be shaken and to prosperity that lasts forever.

> The White Robe of the Heart Invisible
> Is stained with sin, sorrow, pain, and grief.
> No amount of praying or repentance
> Will make it white again.

As long as I walk in ignorance, The
stains of error will cling to me.
Mistakes mark the crooked path of selfishness,
Where suffering and disappointment wait.
Only knowledge and wisdom can purify me
And make my garment clean.
In them lies the water of love,
In them rests peace—undisturbed and eternal. Sin and
repentance are the paths of pain,
But knowledge and wisdom lead to peace.
Through practice,
I'll find where happiness begins,
And how pain and suffering end.
Selfishness will leave, and truth will take its place.
The Changeless One, the Indivisible,
Will live within me and cleanse
The White Robe of the Heart Invisible.

PART 2

THE WAY OF PEACE

1. The power of meditation

Spiritual meditation is the path to becoming one with the Divine. It's like a mystical ladder that connects earth with heaven, from mistakes to truth, from pain to peace. Every saint has climbed this ladder, and every sinner will have to face it someday. Every tired traveler who leaves behind selfishness and the world, and heads toward the Father's Home, must step onto its golden rungs. Without it, you cannot grow into the divine state, experience divine peace, or see the unchanging beauty and pure joys of Truth.

Meditation means thinking deeply about an idea or subject with the goal of truly understanding it. Whatever you focus on constantly, you will not only understand, but you will also become more and more like it because it will become a part of you, it will become who you are. If you keep thinking about selfish or bad things, you will eventually become selfish and bad. If you always think about pure and selfless things, you will surely become pure and selfless.

Tell me what you think about most often and most intensely, where your thoughts naturally go in your quiet moments, and I will tell you whether you are headed for a place of peace or pain, and whether you are becoming like the Divine or something less.

There is a natural tendency to become the very thing you think about most. So, let your meditation be focused on what is above and not below, so that every time you return to it in thought, you will rise higher. Let it be pure, free from any selfish thoughts. In this way, your heart will be cleansed and drawn closer to Truth, instead of becoming defiled and dragged deeper into mistakes.

Meditation, in the spiritual sense that I am talking about, is the key to all growth in spiritual life and understanding. Every prophet, wise person, and savior became who they were through the power of meditation. Buddha meditated on Truth until he could say, "I am the Truth." Jesus thought about the Divine presence within him until he could declare, "I and my Father are One."

Meditation focused on divine realities is the heart and soul of prayer. It is the silent reaching of the soul toward the Eternal. Prayer that asks for things without meditation is like a body without a soul, and it cannot lift your mind and heart above sin and suffering. If you pray every day for wisdom, peace, greater purity, or a deeper understanding of Truth, and these things still seem far away from you, it means you are praying for one thing but thinking and acting in a different way. If you stop this behavior and take your mind off the things that are holding you back from the pure realities you are praying for, you will start to grow into those realities day by day, and eventually, you will become one with them.

Just like someone who wants to achieve anything in the world must be willing to work hard for it, it would be foolish to expect that spiritual rewards will come to you without effort. Only when you start working seriously in the Kingdom of Truth will you be allowed to enjoy the Bread of Life. When you have earned the spiritual rewards you ask for through patient, steady effort, they will not be withheld from you.

If you are really seeking Truth and not just your own satisfaction, if you love Truth more than worldly pleasures or gains, even more than happiness itself, you will be willing to make the effort needed to achieve it.

If you want to be free from sin and sorrow, if you want to experience the pure life you long and pray for, if you want to understand wisdom and knowledge and enter into a state of deep and lasting peace, then come now and begin the path of meditation. Let Truth be the highest goal of your meditation.

At the beginning, it's important to know that meditation is not the same as daydreaming. It is not dreamy or impractical. It is a process of deep, honest thought that leaves only the simple and pure truth. As you meditate in this way, you will no longer try to protect your personal opinions, but instead, forget about yourself and remember only that you are searching for Truth. In this way, you will slowly remove the mistakes you have built around yourself in the past and patiently wait for the Truth to be revealed to you when your mistakes have been cleared away. In the quiet humility of your heart, you will realize that:

"There is a deepest center in us all Where
Truth lives fully; and around, Wall upon
wall, the gross flesh traps it in;
This perfect, clear perception, which is Truth, A
confusing and blinding carnal web
Hides it and creates all mistakes; and knowing,
Is really about opening a way
For the imprisoned splendor to escape,
Rather than bringing in light Supposed
to be outside."

Set aside some time each day for meditation and keep that time
sacred for your purpose. The best time is early in the morning when
everything is peaceful. All natural conditions will then support you:
after the long fast of the night, your passions will be calm, the
worries of the day before will have faded, and your mind, both
strong and rested, will be ready for spiritual learning. One of the first
challenges you'll face will be to shake off laziness and self-indulgence,
and if you don't, you won't be able to move forward, because
spiritual demands are very serious.

To be spiritually awake is also to be mentally and physically awake.
Lazy and self-indulgent people cannot know Truth. A healthy
person who wastes the calm, precious hours of the early morning in
lazy indulgence is not fit to climb the spiritual heights.

Someone whose awakening mind has become aware of its great
possibilities, who is starting to shake off the darkness of ignorance
that covers the world, rises before the stars disappear and, battling
with the darkness inside their soul, strives to see the light of Truth
while the sleeping world continues to dream.

"The heights by great men reached and kept,
Were not attained by sudden flight, But
they, while their companions slept, Were
toiling upward in the night."

No saint, no holy person, no teacher of Truth ever lived who didn't rise early in the morning. Jesus regularly rose early and climbed the mountains alone to pray. Buddha always rose an hour before sunrise to meditate, and all his followers were told to do the same.

If you have to start your day very early and cannot meditate in the morning, try to set aside an hour at night. If even that is impossible because of long and tiring work, don't worry. You can still lift your thoughts toward Truth in moments of rest, or during the idle minutes you now waste on other things. If your work becomes automatic through practice, you can meditate while doing it. The great Christian saint and philosopher Jacob Boehme gained his vast spiritual understanding while working long hours as a shoemaker. In every life, there is time to think, and no one, no matter how busy, is shut out from aspiration and meditation.

Spiritual meditation and self-discipline go hand in hand. You will start by meditating on yourself to understand yourself better. Remember, your goal is to get rid of all your mistakes so you can realize Truth. You will begin to question your motives, thoughts, and actions, comparing them to your ideal, and looking at them with calm honesty. This will help you gain more mental and spiritual balance, which is essential because, without it, people are like helpless straws tossed about on the ocean of life. If you tend to feel hate or anger, meditate on gentleness and forgiveness so that you become aware of how harsh and foolish your behavior is. Then, start thinking about love, gentleness, and forgiveness. As you overcome the lower nature with the higher, you will slowly and quietly come to understand the divine Law of Love and how it applies to all the details of life and behavior. By applying this knowledge to every thought, word, and action, you will grow gentler, more loving, and more divine.

With every mistake, every selfish desire, and every human weakness, meditation is the way to overcome it. As each sin and mistake is removed, a clearer understanding of Truth will shine into your soul.

By meditating, you will constantly strengthen yourself against your only real enemy, your selfish, perishable self, and will establish yourself more firmly in the divine, eternal self that is one with Truth. The result of your meditation will be a calm spiritual strength that will be your support and resting place in the struggles of life. Great is the power of holy thought, and the strength and knowledge you gain in the quiet moments of meditation will guide and protect your soul during times of struggle, sorrow, or temptation.

As you grow in wisdom through meditation, you will let go of your selfish desires, which are unstable, temporary, and cause sorrow and pain. You will stand more firmly on unchangeable principles and will experience heavenly rest.

The purpose of meditation is to gain knowledge of eternal principles, and the power gained from meditation is the ability to trust those principles and become one with the Eternal. The goal of meditation is direct knowledge of Truth, God, and the experience of divine, deep peace.

Let your meditation come from the ethical ground where you now stand. Remember, you will grow into Truth through steady perseverance. If you are a traditional Christian, meditate constantly on the pure and divine excellence of Jesus' character and apply his teachings to your inner life and outward actions so that you become more and more like him. Don't be like those who, refusing to meditate on the Law of Truth or practice the teachings given by their Master, are content with formal worship, clinging to their particular creeds while continuing to live in sin and suffering. Aim to rise above selfish attachments to small gods or religious creeds, above empty rituals and dead ignorance. By walking the path of wisdom, with your mind fixed on spotless Truth, you will not stop until you realize Truth.

A person who meditates seriously first sees Truth from afar, and then comes to realize it through daily practice. Only those who do the Word of Truth can truly understand it. While pure thought allows Truth to be perceived, it is only through practice that it becomes real.

The great Gautama, the Buddha, said, "He who gives himself up to vanity and does not give himself to meditation, forgetting the real purpose of life and chasing after pleasure, will one day envy those who devoted themselves to meditation." He also taught his followers the "Five Great Meditations":

"The first meditation is the meditation of love, where you adjust your heart to wish for the well-being and happiness of all beings, including your enemies.

The second meditation is the meditation of compassion, where you think of all beings in pain, imagining their suffering and worries, so you feel deep compassion for them.

The third meditation is the meditation of joy, where you think of the prosperity of others and share in their happiness.

The fourth meditation is the meditation on impurity, where you think about the bad results of corruption, sin, and disease. You reflect on how brief the pleasure of the moment often is and how serious the consequences can be.

The fifth meditation is the meditation on serenity, where you rise above love and hate, wealth and poverty, power and weakness, and look at your own fate with calmness and peace."

Through these meditations, the Buddha's followers came to know the Truth. But whether you practice these particular meditations or not is not as important as your goal. As long as you seek Truth, as long as you hunger and thirst for righteousness, which is a pure heart and a blameless life, you will make progress. In your meditations, let your heart grow with expanding love until it embraces the entire universe with thoughtful kindness, free from hate, passion, and judgment.

Like a flower opening its petals to receive the morning light, open your soul to the bright light of Truth. Reach higher with your aspirations. Be fearless, and believe in the greatest possibilities.

Believe that a life of absolute gentleness is possible. Believe that a life of perfect purity is possible. Believe that a life of complete holiness is possible. Believe that realizing the highest Truth is possible. Those who believe this climb quickly up the heavenly hills, while those who do not continue to struggle painfully in the dark valleys below.

As you believe, aspire, and meditate, your spiritual experiences will become sweeter and more beautiful, and your inner vision will be filled with glorious revelations. As you come to understand divine Love, divine Justice, divine Purity, and the Perfect Law of Good, or God, your joy will be great and your peace will be deep. Old things will pass away, and all things will become new. The material world, which seems so dense and hard to understand for those who live in error, will become thin and transparent for those who live in Truth, revealing the spiritual universe beyond. Time will cease, and you will live in Eternity. Change and death will no longer cause you anxiety or sorrow, for you will become rooted in the unchanging and will dwell in the very heart of immortality.

> Star of wisdom
> Star that foretold the birth of Vishnu,
> The birth of Krishna, Buddha, and Jesus,
> Told to the wise ones, watching the skies,
> Waiting, searching for your shining
> In the dark night without stars,
> Herald of the coming Kingdom
> Of the righteous ones;
> Teller of the sacred story
> Of God born in the stable of the passions,
> In the manger of the mind-soul;

Silent singer of the secret Of
deep, holy compassion
To the heart burdened by sorrow,
To the soul tired of waiting— Star
of all-surpassing brightness,
You shine again to light the midnight;
You cheer the wise ones
Who watch in the darkness of their creeds,
Tired of the endless struggle
Against the sharp blades of error;
Weary of lifeless, useless idols, Of
the dead forms of religions;
Worn out by waiting for your light; You
have ended their despair;
You have lit up their path;
You have brought back the old Truths
To the hearts of those who watch for you; To
the souls of those who love you,
You speak of joy and gladness,
Of the peace that comes through sorrow. Blessed are those
who can see you,
The weary travelers in the night; Blessed
are those who feel the stirring, Feel the
beating
Of a deep Love awakened within them
By the great power of your light.
Let us learn your lesson truly;
Learn it faithfully and humbly;
Learn it with wisdom, joy, and humility,
Ancient Star of holy Vishnu,
Light of Krishna, Buddha, and Jesus.

2. The two masters, self and truth

In every human soul, two masters are always fighting for control of the heart: the master of self, also known as the "Prince of this world," and the master of Truth, also known as the Father God. The master of self is rebellious and uses tools like passion, pride, greed, vanity, and selfishness, which are weapons of darkness. The master of Truth is gentle and humble, using patience, purity, sacrifice, humility, and love as tools of Light.

This battle takes place in every soul, and just like a soldier cannot fight for two opposing armies at once, each heart is either on the side of self or of Truth. There is no in-between. As Buddha, the teacher of Truth, said, "There is self, and there is Truth. Where self is, Truth cannot be; where Truth is, self cannot be." And Jesus, the Christ, also said, "No man can serve two masters. Either he will hate one and love the other, or he will be loyal to one and despise the other. You cannot serve both God and wealth."

Truth is simple, straightforward, and unchanging. It doesn't allow for any tricks, turns, or compromises. But self is clever, sneaky, and controlled by desires, allowing endless twists and turns. Those who are fooled by self think they can chase after every worldly desire and still hold on to Truth. But lovers of Truth worship Truth by sacrificing self and always watch themselves carefully to avoid worldliness and selfishness.

Do you want to understand and realize Truth? Then you must be ready to sacrifice and give up everything, because you can only see and know Truth in all its glory when every last bit of self is gone.

106

Christ said that anyone who wants to be His disciple must "deny himself daily." Are you ready to deny yourself, give up your desires, your prejudices, and your opinions? If so, you can walk the narrow path of Truth and find the peace that the world cannot reach. The total denial and end of self is the perfect state of Truth, and all religions and philosophies are just different paths to help you reach this supreme goal.

Self denies Truth, and Truth denies self. As you let self die, you will be reborn in Truth. If you hold on to self, Truth will remain hidden from you.

As long as you hold on to self, your path will be filled with difficulties, and you will face pain, sorrow, and disappointment over and over again. But there are no difficulties in Truth, and when you reach Truth, you will be free from all sorrow and disappointment.

Truth itself is not hidden or dark. It is always clear and fully revealed. But the blind and stubborn self cannot see it. Just as the light of day is not hidden from anyone except the blind, the Light of Truth is not hidden from anyone except those who are blinded by self.

Truth is the one true reality in the universe. It is the inner harmony, the perfect justice, and the eternal love. Nothing can be added to it or taken away from it. It doesn't depend on anyone, but everyone depends on it. You cannot see the beauty of Truth if you are looking through the eyes of self. If you are vain, you will see everything through your own vanity. If you are full of desire, your heart and mind will be so clouded by passion that everything will appear distorted. If you are proud and stubborn, you will see nothing in the universe except the importance of your own opinions.

There is one quality that clearly sets the person of Truth apart from the person of self, and that is humility. To be free from vanity, stubbornness, and selfishness, and to consider your own opinions as unimportant, that is true humility.

A person who is full of self thinks his opinions are Truth and everyone else's opinions are wrong. But the humble lover of Truth, who knows the difference between opinion and Truth, looks at everyone with kindness. He doesn't try to defend his own opinions against others, but instead lets go of his opinions so he can love more and show the spirit of Truth. Truth, by its very nature, cannot be fully explained with words; it can only be lived. The more love someone has, the more Truth they possess.

People often get into heated arguments and think they are defending Truth when, in reality, they are just defending their own small interests and temporary opinions. The follower of self fights against others. The follower of Truth fights against himself. Truth is unchanging and eternal. It doesn't depend on your opinion or mine. We can either enter into it, or stay outside, but both defending and attacking it are pointless and only harm ourselves.

People who are trapped by self—those who are passionate, proud, and judgmental—believe their particular belief system or religion is the Truth, and all other beliefs are wrong. They try to convert others with great passion. But there is only one true religion, and that is the religion of Truth. And there is only one mistake, and that is the mistake of self. Truth is not a specific belief. It is an unselfish, pure, and striving heart. A person who has Truth is at peace with everyone and treats everyone with love.

You can easily tell if you are a follower of Truth or a worshiper of self by quietly examining your own mind, heart, and actions. Do you hold on to thoughts of suspicion, hatred, envy, desire, and pride, or do you fight against these thoughts? If it's the first, you are tied to self, no matter what religion you may claim to follow. If it's the second, you are on the path to Truth, even if you don't belong to any religion. Are you passionate, stubborn, always trying to get your own way, self-indulgent, and self-centered? Or are you gentle, mild, unselfish, and willing to give up your own desires? If it's the first, self is your master. If it's the second, Truth is the goal of your heart.

Do you strive for wealth? Do you fight fiercely for your political party? Do you crave power and leadership? Do you show off and praise yourself? Or have you given up the love of money? Have you stopped fighting? Are you content with being unnoticed and taking the lowest place? Have you stopped talking about yourself and stopped feeling proud of yourself? If it's the first, even if you think you worship God, the real god of your heart is self. If it's the second, even if you don't speak the words of worship, you are living with the Most High.

The signs of a person who loves Truth are clear. Listen to the Holy Krishna, as beautifully translated by Sir Edwin Arnold in the "Bhagavad Gita":

"Fearlessness, single-minded pursuit of wisdom,
Open-handed generosity, controlled appetites, piety,
Love for solitude, humbleness, uprightness,
Care not to harm any living thing,
Truthfulness, calmness, forgiveness,
Seeing faults in no one, gentleness toward those who
suffer,
A content heart without strong desires,
A gentle, modest demeanor, mixed with noble patience and
purity,
An unrevengeful spirit, never overvaluing oneself—
These are the signs,
O Prince of India,
Of the one whose feet walk the path of heavenly birth!"

When people are lost in the ways of error and self, and have forgotten the "heavenly birth," which is the state of holiness and Truth, they create artificial standards to judge one another. They make acceptance of their own theology the test of Truth. As a result, people are divided against each other, and there is constant hatred, conflict, and endless suffering.

Reader, do you want to realize the birth into Truth? There is only one way: let self die. Let go of all those desires, appetites, opinions, and prejudices that you have held on to for so long. Let them fall away, and you will find Truth. Stop thinking your own religion is better than all others, and strive to learn the great lesson of love and kindness. Stop holding on to the idea, which causes so much conflict and pain, that the savior you worship is the only savior, and that the savior your brother worships with equal sincerity and passion is a fraud. Instead, work hard to follow the path of holiness, and then you will see that every holy person is a savior of mankind.

Giving up self doesn't just mean giving up outward things. It means giving up inner sins and errors. You don't find Truth by giving up fancy clothes, by giving up wealth, by not eating certain foods, or by speaking sweet words. You find Truth by giving up vanity, by letting go of the desire for wealth, by avoiding self-indulgence, by giving up all hatred, conflict, judgment, and selfishness, and by becoming gentle and pure in heart. Doing the outward things without doing the inward work is hypocrisy, but doing the inward work includes the outward. You can give up the outer world and isolate yourself in a cave or a forest, but you will take all your selfishness with you, and unless you give that up, you will be very miserable and deeply deluded. You can stay right where you are, doing your daily duties, and still renounce the inner enemy, self. Being in the world, but not of the world, is the highest perfection and the greatest victory.

> The renunciation of self is the way to Truth, so,
> "Enter the Path; there is no grief like hate,
> No pain like passion, no deception like the senses;
> Enter the Path; great is the journey
> Of the one who overcomes even one weakness."

As you succeed in overcoming self, you will start to see things in their true relationships. A person driven by passion, prejudice, or personal preference adjusts everything to fit their own bias and only sees their own illusions. A person free from all passion, prejudice, preference, and partiality sees things as they truly are. He has nothing to fight for, nothing to defend, nothing to hide, and no selfish interests to protect. He is at peace. He has realized the deep simplicity of Truth, because this calm, unbiased, and blessed state of mind is the state of Truth. The person who reaches this state lives among the angels and sits at the footstool of the Supreme. Knowing the Great Law, knowing the source of sorrow, knowing the secret of suffering, and knowing the way to freedom in Truth, how could such a person engage in conflict or judgment? Even though he knows the world, blinded by its own illusions and wrapped in the darkness of error and self, cannot see the steady Light of Truth and cannot understand the deep simplicity of the heart that has died or is dying to self, he also knows that when the world's long suffering finally piles up to its breaking point, the burdened soul of the world will seek its final refuge, and when time is fulfilled, every lost soul will return to the fold of Truth. And so, he lives with goodwill toward all, and regards everyone with the same tender compassion that a father has for his wayward children.

People cannot understand Truth because they cling to self, because they believe in and love self, and because they think self is the only reality, when in fact it is the greatest illusion.

When you stop believing in and loving self, you will leave it behind and fly to Truth, finding the eternal Reality.

When people are intoxicated by the pleasures of luxury, vanity, and desire, the thirst for life grows deeper within them, and they fool themselves with dreams of worldly immortality. But when they finally reap what they've sown, and pain and sorrow follow, they will give up self and all its pleasures, and come with aching hearts to the only true immortality—the spiritual immortality in Truth.

People move from evil to good, from self to Truth, through the dark door of sorrow, because sorrow and self are inseparable. Only in the peace and joy of Truth is all sorrow conquered. If you are disappointed because your plans didn't work out, or because someone didn't meet your expectations, it's because you are clinging to self. If you feel regret over your actions, it's because you gave in to self. If you are overwhelmed with embarrassment or frustration because of what someone did or said to you, it's because you are holding on to self. If you are hurt by what has been done to you or said about you, it's because you are walking in the painful way of self. All suffering is caused by self. All suffering ends in Truth. When you have entered into and realized Truth, you will no longer suffer from disappointment, regret, or sorrow, and suffering will leave you.

> "Self is the only prison that can ever bind the soul;
> Truth is the only angel that can open the gates.
> When Truth calls you, rise and follow quickly;
> Its path may lead through darkness, but it ends in light."

The world's sorrow is of its own making. Suffering purifies and deepens the soul, and the deepest sorrow is the doorway to Truth.

Have you suffered much? Have you felt deep sorrow? Have you thought seriously about the meaning of life? If so, you are ready to fight against self and become a disciple of Truth.

People who don't see the need to give up self come up with endless theories about the universe and call them Truth. But you should follow the simple path of righteousness, and you will discover the Truth that doesn't change. Cultivate your heart. Water it constantly with unselfish love and deep compassion, and work hard to keep out any thoughts and feelings that don't align with love. Return good for evil, love for hatred, gentleness for mistreatment, and remain silent when attacked. In this way, you will turn all your selfish desires into the pure gold of Love, and self will disappear into Truth. You will walk blamelessly among men, wearing the easy yoke of humility and clothed in the divine garment of lowliness.

> Come, weary brother!
> Your struggles and striving
> Will end in the heart of the Master of compassion.
> Why do you keep wandering across the desert of self,
> Thirsty for the life-giving waters of Truth?
> Here, at the end of your searching and sinning,
> The stream of Life flows, and
> Love's oasis is green.
> Turn and rest; know the beginning and the end, The
> seeker and the searched, the seer and the seen.
> Your Master is not far away in unreachable mountains,
> Nor hiding in the mirage floating in the air.
> You won't find His magical fountains
> In the paths of despair that lead nowhere.
> Stop searching the dark desert of self,
> Looking for the footsteps of your King.
> If you want to hear the sweet sound of His voice,
> Stop listening to the empty songs of selfishness.

Leave the vanishing pleasures behind;
Give up everything you hold dear.
Come, cast yourself at the shrine of the Innermost, For
the Highest, the Holiest, the Unchanging is there.
Inside your heart, in the silence,
He dwells;
Leave your sorrow, sin, and endless wandering.
Come, bathe in His joy, while He whispers
To your soul the answers it seeks, and wander no more.
So stop, weary brother, your struggles and striving; Find
peace in the heart of the Master of compassion.
Stop wandering in the dark desert of self; Come,
drink from the beautiful waters of Truth.

3. The acquirement of spiritual power

The world is full of people who are always seeking pleasure, excitement, and new things. They want to be entertained, whether through laughter or tears. But they aren't looking for strength, stability, or power. Instead, they chase after weakness and waste the little power they have.

There aren't many men and women of true power and influence because few are willing to make the sacrifices needed to gain power, and even fewer are willing to patiently build their character.

When you're constantly swayed by your changing thoughts and impulses, you are weak and powerless. But when you learn to control and direct those forces, you become strong and powerful. Some people have strong animal instincts and may seem fierce, but that's not real power. The ingredients for power are there, but real power only begins when that fierceness is tamed and controlled by higher intelligence. People can only grow in power by waking up to higher and higher levels of understanding and awareness.

The difference between a weak person and a powerful one isn't in the strength of their personal will (because stubborn people are often weak and foolish), but in their level of awareness and understanding.

Those who chase after pleasure, excitement, and novelty, and those who are driven by impulses and strong emotions, lack the understanding of principles that bring balance, stability, and influence.

A person starts to develop power when they stop giving in to impulses and selfish desires and instead rely on a higher, calmer part of themselves and build their life on a principle. Understanding unchanging principles in your mind is both the source and the secret of the highest power.

After much searching, suffering, and sacrificing, when the light of an eternal principle finally shines on your soul, a divine calm will fill you, and an indescribable joy will lift your heart.

When someone realizes such a principle, they stop wandering and become calm and self-controlled. They stop being a slave to their passions and become a master- builder in shaping their future.

A person who is controlled by selfishness and not by a principle will quickly change when their personal comforts are threatened. They are focused on protecting and defending their own interests and think that any means to do so is justified. They are constantly plotting how to protect themselves from enemies, not realizing that they are their own worst enemy. Such a person's efforts will fall apart because they are separated from Truth and power. Any work based on selfishness will fail, but work built on an unbreakable principle will last.

A person who stands on a principle stays calm, brave, and self-controlled no matter what happens. When they face a test and must choose between their personal comfort and Truth, they will give up comfort and stand firm. Even the threat of pain or death won't stop them. A selfish person sees losing their wealth, comfort, or life as the worst thing that can happen. But a person of principle sees these things as small and unimportant compared to losing their character or losing Truth. To them, the only real tragedy is abandoning Truth.

It's during a crisis that we find out who belongs to darkness and who are the children of Light. It's in times of disaster, ruin, and persecution that we see the difference between those who follow selfishness and those who follow Truth. These times also reveal the men and women of power to the future generations who look back with respect.

It's easy for someone to convince themselves that they believe in principles like Peace, Brotherhood, and Universal Love when they are enjoying their life and possessions. But when those things are threatened, if they suddenly start calling for war, they show that they really believe in selfishness, conflict, and hatred, not peace and love.

The person who does not give up their principles, even when faced with losing everything on earth, including their reputation and life, is the person of power. This is the person whose words and actions will last, the one whom future generations will honor and respect. Jesus endured extreme pain and deprivation because he wouldn't abandon his principle of Divine Love, in which he placed all his trust. Today, the world worships at his pierced feet with deep reverence.

There is no way to gain spiritual power except through inner awakening and enlightenment, which come from realizing spiritual principles. And these principles can only be realized by constantly practicing and applying them.

Take the principle of divine Love. Quietly and patiently think about it with the goal of truly understanding it. Let its light shine on your habits, your actions, your speech, your interactions with others, and even your secret thoughts and desires. As you keep doing this, divine Love will become clearer to you, and your own flaws will stand out more, pushing you to improve. Once you get a glimpse of the unmatched majesty of this eternal principle, you won't be satisfied with your weakness, selfishness, and imperfections. You'll keep striving toward Love until you've given up everything that goes against it and brought yourself into complete harmony with it. And that inner harmony is spiritual power.

Take other spiritual principles like Purity and Compassion and apply them in the same way. Because Truth is so demanding, you won't be able to rest until your soul is free from every stain, and your heart is incapable of any harsh, judgmental, or unkind impulse.

You can only gain spiritual power to the extent that you understand, live by, and trust these principles. And that power will show itself in your life as growing calmness, patience, and inner balance.

Calmness shows superior self-control. Patience is a sign of divine knowledge. And the ability to stay calm through all the distractions and duties of life marks a person of power. "It's easy to live by the world's opinion when you are in the world, and it's easy to live by your own opinion when you're alone, but the great person is the one who stays independent and true to themselves, even in a crowd."

Some mystics believe that perfection in calmness is the source of the power by which so-called miracles happen. And it's true that a person who has gained such perfect control over their inner forces, so that nothing can shake them, must be capable of guiding and directing those forces with great skill.

Growing in self-control, patience, and balance is the same as growing in strength and power. You can only grow this way by focusing your awareness on a principle. Just like a child who tries to walk on their own after many falls and failures finally succeeds, you must enter the path to power by first learning to stand on your own. Break away from the control of customs, traditions, and the opinions of others, until you succeed in walking independently and confidently among people. Trust your own judgment. Be true to your own conscience. Follow the Light within you. All other lights are just distractions. There will be people who tell you that you are foolish, that your judgment is wrong, that your conscience is confused, and that the Light within you is really darkness. Don't listen to them. If what they say is true, then the sooner you, as a seeker of wisdom, discover it for yourself, the better. And you can only find out by testing your own strength. So, continue on your path bravely. Your conscience is yours, and following it makes you a person. Following someone else's conscience makes you a slave. You will fall many times, you will suffer many wounds, and you will face many difficulties for a while, but keep moving forward with faith, believing that victory is ahead. Look for a foundation, a principle, and once you find it, hold on to it. Stand on it until you are firmly fixed and can withstand the storms of selfishness.

Selfishness in any form is wastefulness, weakness, and death. Unselfishness, in its spiritual form, is conservation, power, and life. As you grow in spiritual life and become established on principles, you will become as beautiful and unchanging as those principles. You will taste the sweetness of their immortal essence and realize the eternal and unbreakable nature of the God within.

> No harmful blow can reach the righteous person,
> Standing tall amid storms of hate,
> Defying injury, insult, and curse, Surrounded
> by the trembling slaves of Fate. Majestic in
> the strength of silent power, Serene he
> stands, never shaken or changed; Patient and
> firm in the darkest hour,
> Time bends to him, and he rejects death and doom.
> Wrath's fiery lightnings play around him,
> And hell's deep thunders roar above his head;

But he does not fear, for they cannot harm
The one who stands where earth and time and space are
gone.
Protected by deathless Love, what can he fear? Armored
in unchanging Truth, what loss can he know? Knowing
eternity, he stands unmoved
While shadows pass and come and go.
Call him immortal, call him Truth and Light,
And the glory of prophetic majesty,
For he stands firm in the powers of night, Clothed with the
beauty of divinity.

4. The realization of selfless love

It's said that Michelangelo saw a beautiful statue waiting to be
revealed in every rough block of stone, needing only the master's
hand to bring it to life. In the same way, inside every person lies the
Divine Image, waiting for the master hand of Faith and the chisel
of Patience to bring it out. That Divine Image is revealed as pure,
selfless Love.

Deep within every human heart, even when covered by layers of
hardness, there is the spirit of Divine Love. Its holy and pure
essence is eternal and unchanging. It is the Truth in us; it is what
belongs to the Divine; it is what is real and everlasting. Everything else
changes and passes away, but this Love alone is permanent. To
realize this Love through practicing the highest righteousness, to live
in it and become fully aware of it, is to enter immortality here and
now. It is to become one with Truth, one with God, one with the
heart of everything, and to understand our own divine and eternal
nature.

To reach this Love, to understand and experience it, a person must work persistently and diligently on their heart and mind. They must renew their patience often and strengthen their faith, because there is much to remove and much to accomplish before the Divine Image is revealed in all its beauty.

Anyone who seeks to reach the Divine will be tested to the very limit. This is necessary, because how else can we develop the great patience that brings true wisdom and divinity? At times, all the effort may seem useless, and it will feel like nothing is working. There will be moments when a careless act seems to ruin everything, and just when it seems like the work is nearly done, it might feel like the beautiful form of Divine Love has been destroyed, forcing one to start over. But those who are determined to achieve the highest don't see defeat as real. Every failure is only an appearance, not a reality. Every mistake, every fall back into selfishness, teaches a valuable lesson and brings a small piece of wisdom, helping to move closer to the goal.

> To recognize that: "Out of our mistakes,
> We can build a ladder,
> If we step over each one of them,"

is to begin the journey toward the Divine. For the person who understands this, each mistake is like a dead part of themselves, and they rise over it like stepping stones to higher things.

Once you see your mistakes, sorrows, and struggles as lessons showing you where you are weak and need improvement, you will begin to watch yourself constantly. Every error and every pain will show you what you need to change in your heart to bring it closer to the Divine, closer to Perfect Love. As you move forward, day by day, letting go of your inner selfishness, selfless Love will gradually reveal itself to you. When you start to become more patient and calm, when your irritability, anger, and frustration begin to fade, and when the stronger desires and prejudices no longer control you, then you will know that the Divine is awakening within you. You will feel closer to the eternal Heart, closer to that selfless Love, the possession of which is peace and immortality.

Divine Love is different from human love in one very important way: it has no favoritism. Human love focuses on one person or object and excludes everything else, so when that person or object is lost, the one who loves suffers greatly. Divine Love embraces the whole universe without clinging to any single part. Those who reach it do so by gradually purifying and expanding their human love, burning away all selfish and impure elements. When this happens, they stop suffering. Human love causes suffering because it is narrow, confined, and mixed with selfishness. There is no suffering in Divine Love because it is so pure that it asks for nothing in return.

Human love is necessary as a step toward Divine Love, and no soul can reach Divine Love without first being able to experience deep, intense human love. It is only through human love and human suffering that Divine Love is finally reached.

All human love is temporary, like the forms it clings to, but there is a Love that is everlasting and does not depend on appearances.

All human love is balanced by human hatred, but there is a Love that has no opposite. It is divine, free from all selfishness, and spreads its fragrance equally to all.

Human love is a reflection of Divine Love and brings the soul closer to the reality of that Love, which knows no sorrow or change.

It is right for a mother, holding the small, helpless body of her child, to feel deep sorrow when she sees that child laid in the ground. Her tears and pain remind her of the short-lived nature of the joys and objects of the senses and draw her closer to the eternal and unchanging Reality.

It is right for lovers, brothers, sisters, husbands, and wives to feel deep pain and be filled with darkness when the person they love is taken from them. This suffering teaches them to turn their love toward the invisible Source of all things, where true and lasting satisfaction is found.

It is good for the proud, the ambitious, and the selfish to suffer defeat, humiliation, and hardship. It is through the fires of suffering that the wayward soul begins to reflect on the mystery of life. Only in this way can the heart be softened, purified, and made ready to receive the Truth.

When the pain of sorrow pierces the heart of human love, when loneliness and abandonment overshadow the soul of friendship and trust, that is when the heart turns to the comforting love of the Eternal and finds peace. And whoever turns to this Love will not be left without comfort, will not be pierced by sorrow, and will not be abandoned in the dark hours of trial.

The glory of Divine Love can only be revealed in a heart that has been cleansed by sorrow, and the heavenly state can only be realized when the layers of ignorance and selfishness are stripped away.

Only the Love that asks for no personal gain or reward, that makes no distinctions, and that leaves no pain behind can truly be called divine.

People who cling to selfishness and the empty shadows of wrongdoing often think of Divine Love as something that belongs to a God far out of reach. They see it as something outside of themselves that will always remain distant. It is true that the Love of God is beyond the reach of selfishness, but when the heart and mind are emptied of selfishness, then selfless Love—the supreme Love, the Love of God—becomes a real, living presence within.

This inner realization of holy Love is the same Love of Christ that is often talked about but rarely understood. It is the Love that not only saves the soul from sin but also lifts it above the power of temptation.

But how can someone attain this great realization? The answer that Truth has always given is, "Empty yourself, and I will fill you." Divine Love cannot be known until selfishness is gone, because selfishness denies Love. How can something that is denied also be known? It is only when the stone of selfishness is rolled away from the tomb of the soul that the immortal Christ, the pure Spirit of Love, breaks free from the bonds of ignorance and steps forward in the glory of His resurrection.

You believe that Christ was crucified and rose again. I do not say you are wrong in that belief, but if you refuse to believe that the gentle spirit of Love is crucified every day on the dark cross of your selfish desires, then I say you are wrong in this disbelief, and you have not yet glimpsed, even from a distance, the Love of Christ.

You say that you have experienced salvation in the Love of Christ. But are you saved from your temper, your irritability, your vanity, your personal dislikes, and your judgment and criticism of others? If not, from what have you been saved, and how have you experienced the transforming Love of Christ?

A person who has realized Divine Love becomes a new person. They are no longer controlled by the old forces of selfishness. They are known for their patience, purity, self-control, deep compassion, and unwavering kindness.

Divine Love is not just a feeling or emotion. It is a state of understanding that destroys the power of evil and the belief in evil. It lifts the soul into the joyful experience of the supreme Good. For the truly wise, knowledge and Love are one and cannot be separated.

The whole world is moving toward the full realization of this Divine Love. The universe came into existence for this purpose, and every attempt at happiness, every reaching out for objects, ideas, or ideals, is an effort to experience it. But the world does not understand this Love yet because it is reaching for the fleeting shadow instead of the substance. So suffering and sorrow continue and will continue until the world, taught by its own pains, discovers the Love that is selfless, the wisdom that is calm and full of peace.

This Love, this Wisdom, this Peace—this calm state of mind and heart—can be attained by anyone who is willing to give up selfishness and is ready to understand what giving up selfishness really means. There is no outside force in the universe controlling us, and the strongest chains of fate that bind people are the ones they forge themselves. People are chained to what causes them pain because they choose to be, because they love their chains, because they believe their small, dark prison of selfishness is beautiful and valuable. They are afraid that if they leave that prison, they will lose everything that is real and worth having.

"You suffer from yourselves, no one else forces you, No one else holds you, while you live and die."

The inner power that forged the chains and built the dark, narrow prison can break free whenever it chooses. The soul will choose to do so when it finally sees how worthless its prison is, and when long suffering has prepared it to receive the boundless Light and Love.

Just as shadows follow form and smoke follows fire, so does effect follow cause. Suffering and happiness follow the thoughts and actions of people. There is no effect in the world that doesn't have a hidden or obvious cause, and that cause follows absolute justice. People harvest suffering because in the past, near or far, they planted seeds of wrongdoing. They also harvest happiness as a result of planting seeds of goodness. Let a person meditate on this, strive to understand it, and they will begin to plant only good seeds and clear away the weeds and thorns they once grew in their heart.

The world does not understand selfless Love because it is caught up in the pursuit of its own pleasures and limited by temporary interests, mistaking them for real and lasting things. Consumed by desires of the flesh and burning with pain, it cannot see the pure, peaceful beauty of Truth. Feeding on the empty husks of error and self-delusion, it is shut out from the mansion of all- seeing Love.

Because they do not have this Love, and do not understand it, people create countless reforms that require no inner change. Each person believes their reform will fix the world forever, but they continue to spread evil by keeping it alive in their own hearts. True reform is only that which reforms the human heart, because all evil begins there. The world will not realize the Golden Age of universal happiness until it stops being selfish and learns the lesson of Divine Love.

Let the rich stop despising the poor, and the poor stop condemning the rich. Let the greedy learn to give, and the lustful learn to become pure. Let partisans stop fighting, and the unkind begin to forgive. Let the envious try to be happy for others, and let those who speak badly of others feel ashamed. If people follow this path, the Golden Age will be near. Therefore, the person who purifies their own heart is the world's greatest benefactor.

Even though the world is still far from that Age of Gold, which is the realization of selfless Love, you can enter it now, if you are willing to rise above your selfish self. If you are ready to move from prejudice, hatred, and judgment to gentle and forgiving Love, you may enter.

Where hatred, dislike, and judgment exist, selfless Love cannot be found. It only lives in a heart that has stopped condemning others.

You may say, "How can I love a drunkard, a hypocrite, a thief, or a murderer? I have to dislike and condemn such people." It's true you may not be able to love such people with emotions, but when you say you must dislike and condemn them, it shows you have not yet experienced the great, all-encompassing Love. It is possible to reach a state of inner understanding that allows you to see the causes that led these people to become who they are, to understand their deep suffering, and to know for sure that they will eventually be purified. When you have this understanding, it will be impossible for you to dislike or condemn them, and you will think of them only with calmness and deep compassion.

If you love people and speak kindly about them until they disappoint you or do something you don't like, and then you start disliking them and speaking badly about them, you are not guided by the Love that is of God. If you are constantly judging and condemning others in your heart, then selfless Love is hidden from you.

The person who knows that Love is at the heart of all things, and who has experienced the all-powerful nature of that Love, has no room in their heart for judgment.

People who do not know this Love set themselves up as judges and punishers of others, forgetting that there is an Eternal Judge. When others disagree with their views or methods, they label them as fanatical, unbalanced, or lacking in judgment, honesty, and sincerity. When others agree with them, they praise them as everything that is good. This is how people centered in selfishness behave. But the person whose heart is centered in the supreme Love does not label or judge others in this way. They do not try to convert others to their views or prove the superiority of their methods. Knowing the Law of Love, they live it, and maintain the same calm mind and gentle heart toward everyone. The foolish and the wise, the learned and the unlearned, the selfish and the selfless—all are blessed equally by their peaceful thoughts.

You can only reach this highest understanding, this divine Love, by constantly working on self-discipline and by winning one battle after another over yourself. Only the pure in heart can see God, and when your heart is pure enough, you will experience a New Birth. The Love that never dies, never changes, and never leads to pain or sorrow will awaken within you, and you will find peace.

Those who seek to achieve divine Love are always trying to overcome the urge to judge others, because where there is true spiritual understanding, judgment cannot exist. Only in a heart that is incapable of judgment can Love be perfected and fully experienced.

Christians often judge atheists; atheists make fun of Christians. Catholics and Protestants argue endlessly with each other. The spirit of conflict and hate rules where there should be peace and love.

"He who hates his brother is a murderer," someone who kills the divine Spirit of Love. Until you can look at people of all religions—or no religion—with the same fairness, free from any dislike, and with perfect calmness, you still have work to do to reach that Love, which brings freedom and salvation to those who possess it.

The realization of divine understanding and selfless Love completely destroys the urge to judge others. It clears away all evil and lifts your awareness to a place where Love, Goodness, and Justice are seen as universal, supreme, and undefeatable. Train your mind to think strong, fair, and gentle thoughts. Train your heart in purity and compassion. Train your tongue to stay silent when necessary and speak truthfully and kindly. This will lead you to the path of holiness and peace, and eventually, you will experience immortal Love. By living this way—without trying to convert others—you will persuade them. Without arguing, you will teach. Without seeking fame, wise people will notice you. And without trying to win approval, you will win over people's hearts. Because Love conquers all, it is all-powerful, and the thoughts, actions, and words of Love never die.

To understand that Love is universal, supreme, and all-sufficient; to be freed from evil; to be free of inner conflict; to know that everyone is trying to find the Truth in their own way; to be content, free from sorrow, and at peace—this is joy; this is immortality; this is Divinity; this is the realization of selfless Love.

> I stood by the shore and saw the rocks
> Resist the mighty sea's force.
> I thought about how these rocks had endured
> Countless waves crashing for an eternity, And
> I said, "The waves cannot wear away
> This solid mass, no matter how hard they try." But then I
> saw the sand and pebbles at my feet,
> (Once solid rocks, now broken down)
> Tumbled and tossed where the water meets the shore. I
> saw ancient rocks beneath the waves,
> And I knew the waters had claimed them. I
> saw the great work the waters had done
> With patient softness and endless flow.
> How they brought down the highest cliffs
> To their feet, and laid heavy hills low.
> How soft drops of water
> Could bring down the hardest wall over time.
> And then I knew that hard, resisting sin
> Would eventually give in to Love's soft, constant flow.
> Coming and going,
> Love keeps flowing in
> On the proud rocks of the human soul.
> In time, all resistance will be gone, And
> every heart will give in to it at last.

5. Entering into the infinite

Since the beginning of time, people, despite their physical desires and attachment to earthly things, have always had an inner sense that their material life is limited, temporary, and not fully real. In their quiet moments, they reach out to understand the Infinite and turn with longing toward the eternal peace of the Divine Heart.

Even though they may believe that earthly pleasures are real and satisfying, pain and sorrow constantly remind them that these things are not truly fulfilling. People try to convince themselves that material things can bring them complete happiness, but deep down, they always feel a rebellion against this belief. This rebellion is proof that true satisfaction and lasting peace can only be found in the eternal, the infinite, and the immortal.

This is where faith begins, the foundation of all religion, and the soul of Brotherhood and Love: the belief that humans are spiritually divine and eternal. Even though we are caught up in mortal life and troubled by unrest, we are always striving to connect with our true nature.

The spirit of humanity is inseparable from the Infinite and can only be satisfied with the Infinite. Until we stop wandering in the illusion of material things and return to the reality of the Eternal, we will always carry the weight of pain, and sorrow will always cast a shadow on our path.

Just like the smallest drop of water that is separated from the ocean still contains the qualities of the ocean, so does each person, separated from the Infinite, carry its likeness within. And just as the drop of water must eventually return to the ocean and merge into its depths, so must people, by the law of their nature, return to their source and become one with the Infinite.

The goal of humanity is to become one again with the Infinite. To live in perfect harmony with the Eternal Law is to achieve Wisdom, Love, and Peace. But this divine state cannot be understood by the personal, selfish self. Personality, separateness, and selfishness are all the same thing, and they are the opposite of wisdom and divinity. By giving up selfishness and individuality, we can enter into our divine heritage of immortality and unity with the Infinite.

The selfish, worldly mind sees giving up the self as a terrible loss, but it is actually the greatest blessing and the only real, lasting gain. A mind that is not enlightened about the true nature of life clings to temporary things that have no lasting value. In doing so, it suffers amid the wreckage of its own illusions.

People cling to the pleasures of the flesh as if they would last forever, trying to forget that death is always near and unavoidable. But the fear of death and the loss of what they hold dear darkens even their happiest moments. Their own selfishness follows them like a shadow they cannot escape.

As they gather more material comforts and luxuries, the divine part of them becomes numb, and they sink deeper into a life focused on physical senses. If they are intelligent enough, they may even start to believe that the immortality of the body is a true and unchangeable fact. But when a person is blinded by selfishness, they lose the ability to understand spiritual truth. They confuse what is temporary with what is eternal, what is perishable with what is lasting, and what is false with what is true. This is why the world is filled with beliefs and ideas that have no real basis in human experience. Every physical body contains within itself, from birth, the seeds of its own destruction and must eventually die by the unchangeable law of nature.

What is perishable can never become permanent, and what is permanent can never pass away. Mortality cannot become immortality, and the immortal can never die. The temporary cannot become eternal, nor can the eternal become temporary.

What is false can never become Truth, and Truth can never become false. Humans cannot make the flesh immortal, but by overcoming the desires of the flesh, we can enter the realm of immortality. "God alone has immortality," and only by realizing God's consciousness can we enter into immortality.

Everything in nature, in all its many forms, is changeable, temporary, and will eventually pass away. Only the underlying principle of nature lasts forever. Nature is many and divided, but the principle behind it is One and united. By overcoming our physical desires and selfishness, we overcome nature itself and rise from the personal and temporary to the impersonal, the realm of universal Truth, from which all perishable forms come.

So, people should practice self-denial. They should conquer their physical desires and not let themselves be controlled by luxury and pleasure. They should practice virtue and grow every day into higher and higher virtue until they grow into the Divine. In doing so, they will learn and live the qualities of humility, meekness, forgiveness, compassion, and love, which make up Divinity.

"Good-will gives insight," and only the person who has conquered their selfishness and has goodwill toward all creatures has divine insight and can tell the difference between what is true and what is false. The truly good person is the wise person, the divine person, the enlightened one, the one who knows the Eternal. Where you find constant gentleness, lasting patience, deep humility, kind words, self- control, selflessness, and deep sympathy, look there for the highest wisdom. Seek the company of such a person, for they have realized the Divine, they live with the Eternal, they are one with the Infinite. Do not believe someone who is impatient, given to anger, boastful, clinging to pleasure, unwilling to give up their selfish desires, and who does not practice goodwill and compassion. That person does not have wisdom; their knowledge is useless, and their works and words will pass away because they are based on what is temporary.

Let people abandon selfishness. Let them overcome the world and deny the personal self. Only by following this path can they enter the heart of the Infinite.

The world, the body, and the personality are illusions on the desert of time— temporary dreams in the dark night of spiritual ignorance. Only those who have crossed the desert, those who are spiritually awake, have truly understood the Universal Reality, where all illusions disappear and dreams and delusions are destroyed.

There is one Great Law that demands total obedience, one unifying principle behind all diversity, one eternal Truth that makes all the problems of the world disappear like shadows. To realize this Law, this Unity, this Truth is to enter the Infinite and become one with the Eternal.

To center your life on the Great Law of Love is to find rest, harmony, and peace. To avoid all evil and disharmony, to stop resisting evil, and to follow the calm voice within you without hesitation is to enter the deepest heart of reality. This is how to experience the eternal and infinite principle that will always remain a mystery to the mind that only sees the surface of things. Until this principle is realized, the soul will not find peace. The person who realizes it is truly wise—not with the wisdom of scholars, but with the innocence of a pure heart and a divine spirit.

To realize the Infinite and Eternal is to rise above time, the world, and the body—these things make up the kingdom of darkness. It is to become part of immortality, Heaven, and the Spirit—the Empire of Light.

Entering the Infinite is not just a theory or a feeling. It is a real experience that comes from dedicated inner purification. When you no longer believe that the body is, even remotely, your true self, when you have overcome and purified all desires, when your emotions are calm, and when your mind is steady and at peace, only then will your consciousness become one with the Infinite. Only then will you find childlike wisdom and deep peace.

People often grow old, weary, and troubled by life's problems, eventually passing away without finding answers because they are too focused on their own limitations. By trying to save their personal life, they lose the greater Life of Truth. By clinging to what is perishable, they miss the knowledge of the Eternal.

By giving up the self, all problems are solved. There is no error in the universe that the fire of inner sacrifice will not burn away. There is no problem, no matter how big, that will not disappear like a shadow in the light of selflessness. Problems only exist because of our self-created illusions, and they vanish when we let go of the self. Self and error are the same thing. Error lives in the complexity of confusion, but eternal simplicity is the beauty of Truth.

Love of self keeps people from Truth, and by seeking their own personal happiness, they lose the deeper, purer, and more lasting joy. Carlyle said, "There is in man a higher than love of happiness. He can do without happiness and instead find blessedness. ... Love not pleasure, love God. This is the Everlasting Yes, where all contradictions are solved, and whoever walks and works in this, it is well with him."

The person who has given up their self—the self that people love and hold on to so fiercely—has left behind all confusion and entered a simplicity so deep that the world, trapped in error, may see it as foolishness. But this person has found the highest wisdom and rests in the Infinite. They "accomplish without striving," and all problems disappear before them because they have entered the realm of reality and deal only with the unchanging principles of life. They are filled with wisdom that is far beyond reason, just as reason is beyond mere animal instincts. Having given up their desires, mistakes, opinions, and prejudices, they have gained the knowledge of God. Having let go of the desire for heaven and the fear of hell, they have gained supreme joy and Eternal Life, the Life that bridges life and death and knows its own immortality. By giving up everything, they have gained everything and rest in peace in the arms of the Infinite.

Only those who are so free from the self that they are equally content to live or be forgotten, to exist or be nothing, are ready to enter the Infinite. Only those who have stopped trusting their temporary self and instead trust completely in the Great Law, the Supreme Good, are ready to experience eternal joy.

Such a person no longer feels regret, disappointment, or guilt, because where selfishness has ceased, these sufferings cannot exist. Whatever happens to them, they know it is for their good, and they are content, no longer servants of the self but of the Supreme. They are not affected by the changes of the world. When they hear of wars and rumors of wars, their peace is not shaken. Where others grow angry, cynical, and quarrelsome, they offer compassion and love. Even if appearances say otherwise, they know the world is moving forward, and that,

> "Through its laughing and its weeping,
> Through its living and its keeping,
> Through its mistakes and efforts, weaving in and out of sight,
> To the end from the beginning,
> Through all good and all bad actions,
> Reeled from God's great spool of Progress, runs the golden thread of light."

When a terrible storm is raging, no one is angry because they know it will soon pass. In the same way, when the storms of conflict tear through the world, the wise person looks with Truth and compassion, knowing it will pass and that, from the broken hearts it leaves behind, the immortal Temple of Wisdom will be built.

With sublime patience, endless compassion, deep silence, and pure heart, such a person's presence is a blessing. When they speak, people take their words to heart and rise to greater levels of achievement. This is the person who has entered the Infinite, who has solved the mystery of life through the greatest sacrifice.

> Questioning Life, Destiny, and Truth,
> I went to the dark and confusing Sphinx, Who
> said these strange and wonderful words:
> "Hiding exists only in blinded eyes,
> And only God can see the form of God."
> I tried to solve this hidden mystery
> Through paths of blindness and pain,
> But when I found the Way of Love and Peace,
> Hiding ended, and I was blind no more:
> I saw God with the eyes of God.

6. Saints, sages, and saviors: the law of service

The spirit of Love, which shows itself as a perfect and complete life, is the crown of our being and the highest goal of knowledge on earth.

The amount of truth a person holds is measured by how much they love, and Truth is far from anyone whose life is not guided by Love. People who are intolerant and judgmental, even if they follow a religion, have little truth. But those who are patient, listen calmly to all sides, and lead others to thoughtful and fair conclusions have Truth in its fullest form. The final test of wisdom is this—how does a person live? What kind of spirit do they show? How do they behave when faced with trials and temptations? Many claim to have Truth but are easily overwhelmed by grief, disappointment, and anger, falling apart at the first little challenge. Truth is unchanging, and the more a person stands on Truth, the more they grow in virtue, rise above their emotions, and go beyond their changing personality.

People create temporary beliefs and call them Truth, but Truth cannot be put into words or systems—it goes beyond intellect. Truth can only be experienced through action and seen in a pure heart and a perfect life.

So, who has Truth in the midst of all the endless noise of different beliefs and ideas? The one who lives it. The one who practices it. The person who has risen above the noise by overcoming their own self, who no longer gets involved in arguments but remains quiet, calm, and at peace. This person is free from all conflict, bias, and judgment, and gives to all the unselfish Love that comes from the divinity within them.

A person who is patient, calm, gentle, and forgiving in all situations shows the Truth. Truth will never be proven by arguments or books. If people cannot see Truth in patience, forgiveness, and compassion, no amount of words will convince them.

It is easy for passionate people to be calm and patient when they are alone or in peaceful situations. It is also easy for unkind people to be kind when others treat them well. But the one who stays patient and calm through all trials, who remains gentle and humble under the toughest circumstances, is the only one who truly has the spotless Truth. These high virtues belong to the Divine and can only be shown by someone who has reached the highest wisdom, has given up selfishness, and has come into harmony with the unchangeable Law.

So, people should stop arguing about Truth and instead think, say, and do things that create harmony, peace, love, and goodwill. They should practice virtues of the heart and humbly and diligently search for the Truth that frees the soul from all error and sin, from everything that darkens the human heart and clouds the path of wandering souls.

There is one great Law that embraces everything and is the foundation of the universe—the Law of Love. It has been called by many names at different times and in different places, but behind all these names, the same unchanging Law can be seen by those who know Truth. Names, religions, and personalities fade away, but the Law of Love remains. To know this Law and live in harmony with it is to become immortal, unbeatable, and indestructible.

It is because of the soul's effort to understand this Law that people come back again and again to live, suffer, and die. And once the Law is understood, suffering ends, personality disappears, and physical life and death lose their hold because consciousness becomes one with the Eternal.

The Law is completely impersonal, and its highest expression is Service. When a purified heart understands Truth, it is then called to make the greatest and holiest sacrifice—the sacrifice of the well-earned enjoyment of Truth. This sacrifice is what brings a soul, freed by divinity, back to live among people, clothed in a human body, willing to live among the lowliest and be a servant to all. The humble spirit shown by the world's saviors is a sign of their divinity. The person who has destroyed their selfishness and become a living example of the eternal, boundless Spirit of Love is the only one who deserves the lasting worship of future generations. The one who humbles themselves with divine humility, which is more than just the loss of self— it is the giving of unselfish love to everyone—is lifted up beyond measure and given spiritual power in the hearts of people.

All great spiritual teachers denied themselves personal luxuries, comforts, and rewards. They turned away from worldly power and taught the timeless Truth, which is limitless and impersonal. Compare their lives and teachings, and you will see the same simplicity, the same self-sacrifice, humility, love, and peace, both in how they lived and what they taught. They all taught the same eternal Principles, which, when understood, destroy all evil. Those who are seen as the saviors of humanity are examples of the Great impersonal Law, free from passion and prejudice. Since they had no opinions to push or doctrines to defend, they never tried to convert others or make new followers. Living in the highest Goodness and Perfection, their only goal was to uplift humanity by showing that Goodness in thought, word, and deed. They stand between people and God, serving as examples of salvation for those trapped in selfishness.

People who are caught up in themselves cannot understand the impersonal Goodness and deny divinity to all saviors except their own. They bring in personal hatred and arguments about doctrine, defending their own views with passion while seeing others as heathens or infidels. In doing so, they destroy the unselfish beauty and holiness of the lives and teachings of their own Masters. Truth cannot be limited to any person, school, or nation. When selfishness steps in, Truth is lost.

The glory of the saint, the sage, and the savior is that they have reached the deepest humility and the highest unselfishness. By giving up everything, even their own personality, all their actions become holy and lasting because they are free from any trace of self. They give without thinking about receiving. They work without regretting the past or worrying about the future, and they never seek reward.

When a farmer has worked the land, planted seeds, and done all he can, he knows he must now trust nature and wait patiently for the harvest. He knows that no amount of waiting or hoping will change the outcome. In the same way, the person who has realized Truth goes out as a sower of goodness, purity, love, and peace without expecting anything in return, knowing that the Great Law brings about the harvest in its own time.

People who don't understand the simple, unselfish heart see their savior as a special miracle, something separate from the world. They think the savior's goodness is impossible for anyone else to reach. This belief in the unattainable goodness of humanity weakens effort and traps people in sin and suffering. But Jesus "grew in wisdom" and was "perfected by suffering." What Jesus

144

became, he grew into. What Buddha became, he also grew into. And every holy person became such through constant effort and self-sacrifice. Once you recognize this and realize that, through watchful effort and perseverance, you too can rise above your lower nature, great and glorious possibilities will open before you. Buddha vowed not to give up until he reached perfection, and he achieved it.

What saints, sages, and saviors have accomplished, you can accomplish too, if you follow the same path of self-sacrifice and service to others.

Truth is very simple. It says, "Give up yourself," "Come to Me (away from everything that harms), and I will give you rest." No amount of commentary can hide this from a heart that seeks Righteousness. You don't need special knowledge to understand it; it can be known without learning. No matter how much people try to disguise it, the beautiful simplicity and clarity of Truth remain unchanged, and an unselfish heart can enter into its shining radiance. Truth is not realized by making complicated theories or building speculative philosophies. It is realized by weaving the web of inner purity and building the Temple of a spotless life.

The person who walks this holy path begins by controlling their desires. This is virtue and the beginning of sainthood, and sainthood is the start of holiness. The completely worldly person gives in to all their desires and practices no more restraint than the law requires. The virtuous person controls their desires. The saint fights against selfish and impure thoughts in their heart, while the holy person is free from all impure thoughts, and goodness comes as naturally to them as a flower's scent and color. The holy person is divinely wise; they alone know Truth in its fullness and have entered into lasting peace. For them, evil no longer exists; it has disappeared in the universal light of the All-Good. Holiness is the sign of wisdom. Krishna said to Prince Arjuna:

"Humility, truthfulness, and kindness,
Patience and respect, honor for the wise,
Purity, self-control, and sacrifice,
Understanding the truth about pain
In birth, death, age, disease, suffering, and sin;
A heart always calm in good or bad fortune
… A strong effort to understand the highest soul, And
the grace to know the great gain of reaching it— This
is true wisdom, Prince!
And anything else is ignorance!"

Whoever fights against their own selfishness and replaces it with all-embracing love is a saint, whether they live in a small home or among riches, whether they preach or live quietly.

To someone just beginning to strive for higher things, a saint like St. Francis of Assisi or St. Anthony is a beautiful and inspiring example. To the saint, the vision of a wise person who has conquered sin and sorrow is equally inspiring. This sage, sitting serene and holy, is free from regret, and even temptation no longer reaches them. But even the sage is drawn by an even more glorious vision—the savior, who uses their knowledge in selfless acts and shares their divinity by giving themselves to the suffering, aspiring hearts of humanity.

This is true service—to forget oneself in love for all, to lose oneself in working for the good of all. O foolish person, who thinks your many works can save you, who loudly talks about yourself, your works, and your sacrifices, and who magnifies your own importance—know this: even if your fame spreads across the world, all your works will come to nothing, and you will be counted lower than the least in the Kingdom of Truth!

Only work that is done without selfishness will last. The works of self are weak and will perish. Where humble duties are done with joyful sacrifice and without self- interest, there is true service and lasting work. Where great deeds, even if they appear successful, are done for selfish reasons, there is ignorance of the Law of Service, and that work will fade away.

The world is meant to learn one great lesson, the lesson of complete unselfishness. The saints, sages, and saviors of all time have taken on this task and lived it out. All the world's Scriptures are written to teach this one lesson, and all the great teachers have repeated it. It is too simple for the world, which, in rejecting it, stumbles along the complicated path of selfishness.

A pure heart is the goal of all religion and the beginning of divinity. To seek this Righteousness is to walk the Way of Truth and Peace, and whoever walks this path will soon see Immortality, which goes beyond birth and death, and will know that in the Divine order of the universe, even the smallest effort is not wasted.

The divinity of Krishna, Buddha, or Jesus is the final achievement of complete selflessness, the end of the soul's journey through material life. The world's journey will not be finished until every soul has become like them and has entered into the joyful realization of its own divinity.

> Great glory rewards the heights of hope reached through
> struggle;
> Bright honor crowns the wise and mighty work of those
> who have done much;
> Fair riches come to those who strive for wealth with effort
> and intelligence.
> And fame remembers the names of those who create with
> genius and skill.
> But greater glory waits for the one who, in the peaceful fight
> Against selfishness and wrong, embraces the life of
> sacrifice;
> And brighter honor surrounds the one who, despite the
> scorn
> Of those who worship themselves, accepts the crown of
> thorns.
> Fairer, purer riches come to the one who strives
> To walk in love and truth, making human lives better.
> And the one who serves humanity well trades fleeting fame
> For Eternal Light, Joy, Peace, and robes of heavenly flame.

7. The realization of perfect peace

In the outside world, there is constant turmoil, change, and unrest, but deep inside everything is a place of peace where the Eternal lives.

Humans experience this duality as well, having both the surface-level turmoil and the deep, unchanging place of Peace inside them.

Just like the deep ocean stays calm even in the wildest storms, there are calm, holy depths in a person's heart that the storms of sin and sorrow can never disturb. Finding this inner silence and living in it brings true peace.

While there's chaos in the outside world, perfect harmony exists at the heart of the universe. The human soul, torn apart by strong emotions and grief, instinctively reaches toward the peace of a sinless state. Finding this state and living in it is peace. Hatred tears people apart, causes persecution, and leads nations into wars. Yet, even though most don't fully understand it, people still hold onto a belief in a Perfect

Love. Finding this Love and living in it is peace.

This inner peace, this silence, this harmony, this Love, is the Kingdom of Heaven, which is hard to reach because few are willing to let go of themselves and become like little children again.

> "Heaven's gate is very narrow and small,
> It can't be seen by foolish men
> Blinded by the empty promises of the world;
> Even those who see the way
> Find the door locked, Its heavy bolts
> Are pride, passion, greed, and lust."

People cry for peace where there is no peace, only conflict, unease, and fighting. Without the wisdom that comes from giving up the self, there can be no lasting peace.

The peace that comes from social comfort, temporary pleasure, or winning in life is fleeting and burns away when trials come. Only the Peace of Heaven lasts through all trials, and only a selfless heart can know this Peace.

Holiness is the only thing that brings eternal peace. Self-control leads to it, and growing wisdom lights the way. You get a taste of this peace when you start on the path of virtue, but you only fully realize it when the self disappears, and you live a life free of stains.

> "This is peace,
> To conquer love of self and desire for life,
> To tear deep passions from the heart And
> quiet the inner struggle ."

If you want to find the Light that never fades, the Joy that never ends, and the tranquility that can't be disturbed, if you want to leave your sins, sorrows, worries, and confusion behind forever, if you want to experience this glorious Life, then conquer yourself. Bring every thought, every impulse, and every desire into obedience to the divine power within you. There is no other way to peace. If you refuse to walk this path, all your prayers and strict religious rituals will be useless. Neither gods nor angels can help you. Only the one who overcomes receives the white stone of the renewed life, on which is written the New and Sacred Name.

Step away, for a while, from outside things, from the pleasures of the senses, from intellectual arguments, and from the noise and excitement of the world. Withdraw into the deepest part of your heart, and there, free from selfish desires, you will find deep silence, a holy calm, and blissful rest. If you stay in that holy place for a while and meditate, the perfect eye of Truth will open within you, and you will see things as they really are. This holy place inside you is your true and eternal self; it is the divine part of you. Only when you identify with it can you be said to be truly "clothed and in your right mind." It is the home of peace, the temple of wisdom, and the dwelling place of immortality. Without this inner resting place, this Mount of Vision, there can be no true peace or knowledge of the Divine. If you can stay there for a minute, an hour, or a day, you can stay there forever.

Your sins, sorrows, fears, and worries are your own, and you can either cling to them or let them go. You hold onto your unrest by choice; you can choose peace just as easily. No one else can give up sin for you—you have to give it up yourself. The greatest teacher can only walk the way of Truth for themselves and point it out to you; you have to walk it on your own. You can only find freedom and peace through your own efforts by letting go of whatever binds your soul and destroys your peace.

The angels of divine peace and joy are always near, and if you don't see or hear them, it's because you shut yourself off from them and choose instead to keep the spirits of evil inside you. You are what you choose to be, what you wish to be, and what you prefer to be. You can start purifying yourself and reach peace, or you can refuse and stay in suffering.

Step aside, then. Come out of the busy, feverish life; away from the burning heat of selfishness, and enter the place of inner rest, where the cool breezes of peace will calm, renew, and restore you.

Leave the storms of sin and pain behind. Why stay troubled and tossed about when the Peace of God is yours?

Give up all selfish desires; give up the self, and the Peace of God will be yours! Subdue the animal nature inside you; overcome every selfish impulse and every negative thought. Turn the base metals of your selfishness into the pure gold of Love, and you will realize the Life of Perfect Peace. In doing this, you will, while still living in the flesh, cross the dark waters of mortality and reach the Shore where the storms of sorrow never come, and where sin, suffering, and uncertainty cannot touch you. Standing on that Shore—holy, compassionate, fully aware, and filled with endless gladness—you will understand that

> **"The Spirit was never born, and it will never die; There was never a time it was not; beginnings and endings are dreams;**
> **The Spirit is birthless, deathless, and changeless forever;**
> **Death has never touched it, even though the body seems dead."**

You will understand the meaning of Sin, Sorrow, and Suffering and see that their end is Wisdom. You will understand the cause and purpose of existence.

With this realization, you will enter into rest, for this is the bliss of immortality, the unchanging gladness, the perfect knowledge, undefiled Wisdom, and undying Love. This, and this alone, is the realization of Perfect Peace.

O you who would teach men of Truth!
Have you passed through the desert of doubt? Have
you been cleansed by the fires of sorrow? Have the
fiends of opinion been cast out
Of your heart? Is your soul so pure
That no false thought can ever live there?
O you who would teach men of Love!
Have you passed through the place of despair?
Have you cried through the dark night of grief?
Is your heart, now free from sorrow and care, So
gentle that it moves
With pity when you see wrong, hate, and struggle?
O you who would teach men of Peace! Have
you crossed the wide ocean of strife? Have
you found on the Shores of Silence The
release from all the unrest of life?
Has your heart let go of all striving,
Leaving only Truth, Love, and Peace behind?

* * *

The End

Thank you for Reading

You've Just Read a Piece of the Greatest Library Ever Rebuilt

Thank you for reading.

This book is one of thousands we're restoring, reimagining, and translating as part of the **Modern Library of Alexandria** — a global movement to preserve and share humanity's most important ideas.

What was once lost to fire and time is now rising again — not just as memory, but as living, breathing knowledge, freely accessible to all.

What You Can Do Next:

- **Keep Reading.**

  Discover more legendary works — in beautiful print, audiobook, or digital form — at LibraryofAlexandria.com.

- **Build Your Own Library.**

  Every title is available as a paperback, hardcover, or collectible boxset — at true printing cost. Craft a personal library worthy of display.

- **Spread the Light.**

  Share this book. Tell others about the movement. Help us translate every timeless work into every language, so no reader is ever left behind.

By finishing this book, you've already taken part in something extraordinary.

Join us at LibraryofAlexandria.com

Together, we're rebuilding the greatest library the world has ever known.

With appreciation,
The Modern Library of Alexandria Team

Visit:

www.libraryofalexandria.com

Or scan the code below:

www.ingramcontent.com/pod-product-compliance
Lightning Source LLC
Chambersburg PA
CBHW011344090426
42741CB00018B/3437